Warmest regards

[signature]

2/21/92

Democracy and Foreign Policy

Democracy and Foreign Policy

THE FALLACY OF
POLITICAL REALISM

MIROSLAV NINCIC

COLUMBIA UNIVERSITY PRESS

NEW YORK

COLUMBIA UNIVERSITY PRESS
NEW YORK   OXFORD

Copyright © 1992 Columbia University Press

Library of Congress Cataloging-in-Publication Data

Nincic, Miroslav.
    Democracy and foreign policy: the fallacy of political realism /
Miroslav Nincic.
        p.   cm.
    Includes bibliographical references and index.
    ISBN 0-231-07668-1
    1. United States—Foreign relations—1945–1989. 2. United States—
Foreign relations—1989- I. Title.
E840.N55   1992
327.73—dc20   91-37783
                                                                    CIP

                            ∞
Casebound editions of Columbia University Press books are Smyth-sewn
    and printed on permanent and durable acid-free paper.

Printed in the United States of America
        c 10   9   8   7   6   5   4   3   2   1

TO DAVID AND DONNA

CONTENTS

ACKNOWLEDGMENTS

Edward H. Alden, Cecil V. Crabb, Jr., Ole R. Holsti, Bruce W. Jentleson, and Donald Rothchild read all or most of the manuscript and generously provided comments and advice. Bruce Cronin, of New York University, and Roger Rose, of the University of California, Davis, were diligent and helpful research assistants.

Democracy and Foreign Policy

Chapter 1

THE TERMS OF THE DEBATE

Domestic affairs and foreign relations are intimately linked. Often both are but different aspects of the same thing.   —Charles Beard

This book addresses the intersection of democracy, as defined in the American political tradition, and U.S. foreign policy. It argues that by misdirecting our gaze, we have misdiagnosed the major points of friction between the nation's internal political arrangements and its external relations, which has led us to incorrect and often harmful assumptions about the appropriate domestic setting for the conduct of foreign affairs. Accordingly, the book seeks to provide a fuller and more accurate rendering of the interplay between national political norms and international conduct.

That the fabrics of internal politics and foreign policy are interwoven is an important but not a novel idea, for their common threads have been apparent in ancient as well as modern times. Thucydides noted that the manner in which Greek city-states conducted their mutual relations was shaped by pressures from within them, and he observed that the policies they directed toward each other were often intended to produce a domestic rather than external effect.[1] Similarly, Rome's foreign wars of the fourth and fifth centuries B.C. have been partly attributed to expansionary pressures arising from "surplus population and unsatisfactory economic conditions among the rural classes."[2] At the same time, the fact that the plebeian class shared the dangers of these wars equally with the patricians contributed to the expansion of plebeian political rights.[3]

The interdependence of external and internal politics has certainly been felt in the United States. Occasionally, foreign policy has reverberated internally, as with the contention surrounding President Washington's decision to maintain America's neutrality in the war between Britain and France, or with the domestic ado caused by the Jay Treaty. Occasionally too, foreign policy has experienced the consequences of internal political gamesmanship, as witnessed by the fate of President Wilson's attempts to bring the country into the Treaty of Versailles and the League of Nations.[4] President Kennedy's national security adviser and former Harvard historian McGeorge Bundy, when asked how his experience in government had affected his understanding of foreign policy, emphasized his new appreciation of the hold that domestic politics has on the conduct of external affairs.[5]

Though we understand many things about the link between internal and external politics, isolated strands of the relationship are recognized more easily than the overall patterns that endow them with meaning. In particular, and beyond platitudes, we perceive only dimly the effect of a country's political system, of its norms of conduct and principles of power distribution, on the content of its foreign affairs.[6] Nor do we have an adequate grasp of the extent to which political systems themselves are molded by external ambitions and the tools employed in their pursuit.

The idea that the principles of liberal democracy, as the term is understood in the Western world, should apply to foreign as well as domestic affairs is a recent one. During the greater part of European history, the costs and benefits of external relations were borne or enjoyed by monarchs and their coteries rather than by the population as a whole. As the societal impact of foreign policy was, during many recent centuries, quite modest—more so, in fact, than during antiquity—the issue of societal participation in, or control over, its making did not arise. The classical theorists of democracy usually segregated the foreign and domestic realms, feeling that they had no necessary bearing on each other. John Locke observed that "what is to be done in reference to foreigners, depending much upon their actions, and the variations of designs and interests, must be left in great part to the prudence of those who have this power committed to them, to be managed to the best of their skill for the advantage of the commonwealth."[7] The assumption was that even if the masses were concerned with foreign policy, they lack the knowledge and skills needed to guide its conduct.

Approximately one century later, Jean Jacques Rousseau, whose conception of democracy was in some ways more ambitious than Locke's, maintained that "what matters principally to every citizen is the observance of the laws internally, the maintenance of private property, and the security of the individual. As long as all goes well with regard to these three points, let the government negotiate and make treaties with foreign powers."[8] Not only were the people deemed ill-equipped to meddle in foreign affairs, no reason was seen why they should desire to do so.

The U.S. Constitution affirmed the principles of congressional participation and executive accountability in external policymaking well before this was more generally considered desirable, but not everyone agreed this was a good idea. Writing in the early 1830s, Alexis de Tocqueville doubted that American democracy was suited to the rigors of international politics. His own observations included classical balance of power politics, Europe's and Russia's tradition of imperial expansion, the wars of the French revolution, and the hegemonic pretensions of the Concert of Europe. With few illusions about the character of international society, and many qualms regarding America's ability to deal with other nations, he explained, in a much-quoted passage, that

> foreign politics demand scarcely any of those qualities which are peculiar to a democracy; they require, on the contrary, the perfect use of almost all those in which it is deficient. Democracy is favorable to the increase in the internal resources of the state, it diffuses the respect for law in all classes of society: all these are advantages which have only an indirect influence over the relations which one people bears to another. But a democracy can only with great difficulty regulate the details of an important undertaking, persevere in a fixed design, and work out its execution in spite of serious obstacles. It cannot combine its measures with secrecy or await their consequences with patience.[9]

Because of America's isolationism prior to World War I, the issue of the compatibility of international pursuits with the domestic political structure did not appear pressing enough to merit much debate; subsequently however, the problem presented itself more urgently. The war had been justified as a crusade to "make the world safe for democracy"; included among its consequences were the introduction of constitutional democracy in a number of nations (mainly in Central Europe) that had known nothing but autocracy, and the expansion of democratic principles in countries with a long experience of this form of government (as with the extension of suffrage in Great Britain). The worldwide strengthening of democracy's roots affected conceptions of how foreign policy should be made. Moreover, it was felt that the war itself had been the product of the shortsightedness and self-serving ambitions of political elites to which the public might have put a stop, if only it had been consulted. The first of Woodrow Wilson's Fourteen Points, which called for "open covenants of peace, openly arrived at," and demanded that "diplomacy shall proceed always frankly and in public view," must be understood in this light.

As the scope of democracy has expanded, the question of its compatibility with areas of policy that it was not previously assumed to cover has become more pressing. In recent decades, U.S. foreign policy has been almost wholly absorbed with confronting the challenge to democracy represented by the Soviet Union and the ideology it stood for. In light of this endeavor, questions have been raised about the compatibility of the vehicle with the purpose. The suspicion presented itself that a democracy might not be able to muster the will and tenacity needed to compete with a highly committed and organized foe. Although these worries were voiced most loudly at the height of the Cold War, the wave of hostility that followed the short-lived detente of the seventies saw renewed qualms about the ability of democracies to sustain a conflictual purpose. More recently, as the major national challenges have shifted from military security to the maintenance of international economic leadership, the ability of the political system to sustain the necessary effort and sacrifices has again been questioned. Paul Kennedy has suggested that it may be "in the cultural and domestic political realms, that the evolution of an effective overall American policy to meet the twenty-first century will be subjected to the greatest test."[10] Offering a more optimistic assessment of the economic challenges facing the United States, Joseph Nye has nevertheless wondered whether its "political sclerosis" will not be an obstacle to confronting them.[11]

An Introduction to Theoretical Confusion

Though most Americans would claim that theirs is the best form of government from both the individual and societal point of view, the consensus begins to fray when it comes to judging U.S. democracy's virtues at confronting external challenges. Contemporary political science provides little in the way of a framework within which to address the topic, but it does have a less direct contribution to make— for the light that it sheds on the behavior and predispositions of various segments of the American polity illuminates much about democracy and foreign policy as well. At the same time, political realism, the dominant doctrine of foreign policy scholarship, has made numerous assertions in this area. Taken together, science and doctrine provide a prism through which democracy's bearing on the sagacity and effectiveness of foreign policy can be viewed.

In the absence of an established theoretical foundation on which to build our investigation, we will examine the major assertions that have been made on the topic—not only to trace the contours of observers' concerns but to highlight the considerable range of opinion on these issues.

The Impact of Democracy on Foreign Policy

Roughly, qualms can be divided into two sorts. The first, which revolves around the theme of *disruption from below*, dwells on the harmful consequences of the popular pressures to which democratic governments must respond and that are assumed to drive foreign policy off the path of cool reason and calculated reflection needed to deal with an anarchical world. This is the rubric under which the bulk of misgivings seem to fall, and in terms of which nondemocratic regimes are thought to enjoy their principal advantage.

A second group of concerns, in no way incompatible with the first although less often expressed, focuses on what might be termed *derailment from above*. It addresses problems originating within the upper echelons of political power and the very structure of democratic political authority that include the manner in which foreign policy authority is apportioned within the government—especially, in the U.S. case, as a consequence of political pluralism and the separation of powers. Possible problems also include the pattern of incentives by which democratic leaders are driven—at election time in particular—that are not always thought conducive to wisdom and foresight in international affairs.

Disruption from Below and the Legacy of Realpolitik

Although views of external and domestic politics are not bound by a logically inevitable link, a connection is often established between the nature of the global system and the domestic political arrangements through which it is most suitably dealt with. As a general rule, the less benign the perceived character of global society, and the more international existence is deemed an anarchic struggle for power among nations, the less tolerant is the perceiver of domestic pluralism and popular participation of the conduct of foreign relations. To some degree, this follows from the primacy of diplomacy and national security over domestic principles when the international environment appears hostile. In a less easily apparent way, it stems from assumptions about the consequences of participatory policymaking for the wisdom with which external relations are likely to be conducted.

The belief in the primacy of foreign policy has a distinguished pedigree, predating contemporary realist thought. It is found in Thucydides' reflections on the history of the Peloponnesian war.[12] It is present in Machiavelli's writing, where it appears as a major foundation of his admiration for strong government.[13] Particularly explicit affirmations of the primacy of foreign policy have been provided in German historiography and political thought, most influentially in the writings of Leopold von Ranke who, regarding the nation state as an instrument of both power and morality (the former being the essential condition for the latter), placed successful participation in international power contests near the top of his hierarchy of necessary national pursuits.[14] Writing in Ranke's wake, Friedrich Meinecke furnished further elaboration of the necessary subordination of domestic to foreign affairs,[15] arguing that the internal order of the state must respond to the compulsions of international power politics, if the independence of each nation state is to be preserved. Though advocating constitutional government, he preferred a constitution that would insulate the management of international affairs from the exercise of the citizenry's political prerogatives: Foreign policy being the most important and delicate of the state's missions, it should not be constrained by mass sentiment. While Meinecke's views on the subject were tempered in his later work, much of his early thinking encouraged the proposition that, where external relations are concerned, the best system is a form of dictatorship based on trust.

Common to these authors is a belief in the dominant role of power in world politics and a commitment to strong government in the conduct of foreign policy—themes currently reflected in the school of political realism (realpolitik), whose influence has dominated U.S. scholarship of the postwar era.[16] The overlap between realists is obviously imperfect, and no brief summary can capture the richness and nuances of this body of thought.[17] Nevertheless, a focus on Hans J. Morgenthau is a good point of departure, since his *Politics Among Nations* has, directly or indirectly, shaped the course of much subsequent writing in this tradition and since he offers a particularly clear statement of the dangers of disruption from below.[18]

Morgenthau doubted that political systems subjected to the vagaries of public opinion could adhere to the requirements of political realism in their international conduct. Building on some of de Tocqueville's concerns, he argued,

> Thinking required for the successful conduct of foreign policy can be diametrically opposed to the rhetoric and action by which the masses and their representatives are likely to be moved. The peculiar qualities of the statesman's mind are not always likely to find a favorable response in the popular mind. The statesman must think in terms of national interest, conceived as power among other powers. The popular mind, unaware of the fine distinctions of the statesman's thinking, reasons more often than not in the simple moralistic and legalistic terms of absolute good and absolute evil. The statesman must take the long view, proceeding slowly and by detours, paying with small losses for great advantage; he must be able to temporize, to compromise, to bide his time. The popular mind wants quick results; it will sacrifice tomorrow's real benefit for today's apparent advantage.[19]

Thus, it can be adduced, the flexible cynicism and long-term perspective required by international politics is ill-suited to the callow and ephemeral impulses as well as the general ignorance by which masses are driven. While recognizing that democratic leaders cannot be indifferent to domestic sentiment, Morgenthau recommended that they seek compromises between the claims of foreign policy and the public's inclinations—never yielding too much to the latter, but never alienating the public to the point of undermining domestic support for needed policies.[20] Most important, he cautioned leaders against being passive respondents to national moods, urging them to mold popular feelings in accordance with the true national interests, since public opinion "is not a static thing to be discovered and classified by public opinion polls as plants are by botanists, but . . . a dynamic, ever changing entity to be continuously created and recreated by informed and responsible leadership."[21]

Whether or not the leadership effectively manages its public, it follows from this perspective that a "natural weakness" of democratic government is "in the field of foreign policy."[22] In the more apocalyptic view, democracy's principal virtues may be the cause of its ultimate undoing. A major problem in the eyes of some is that democracies tend to be sluggish on the uptake, that they do not react promptly to foreign challenges and that, when they do react, they rarely do so in a measured manner. Walter Lippmann, also an influential realist, had similar qualms about the consequences of a foreign policy driven by public moods. He felt that public opinion encouraged the conditions that led to World War II: by imposing a vindictive settlement on Germany in 1918 and then by refusing to react promptly when German resentment produced Nazism and fueled Hitler's aggressive expansionism.[23] Once war became inevitable, however, an exaggerated image of the German threat was needed to shake the popular mind from its torpor: "It seemed impossible to wage the war energetically except by inciting the people to paroxysms of hatred and to utopian dreams. . . . The war could be popular only if the enemy was altogether evil and the Allies very nearly perfect. This mixture of envenomed hatred and furious righteousness made a public opinion that would not tolerate the calculated compromises that durable settlements demand."[24]

In a somewhat related vein, many of the neoconservative opponents of accommodation with the Soviet Union in the 1970s lamented the "culture of appeasement" to which, in their view, democracies in general and the United States in particular had fallen prey, and which stemmed from the lethargy to which public moods are prone.

Misgivings about the consequences of public pressures for U.S. foreign policy are applied by extension, though in more mitigated form, to activities of the public's legislative representatives. Propelled from the ranks of the public into the councils of government, they are often assumed to project the ignorance and caprices of the populace onto decisions of major national and international consequence. Indeed, according to Morgenthau, legislators represent an even greater threat to wise foreign policy than does inchoate public sentiment.[25] He implies that foreign policy shaped by parliamentary institutions, like that driven by public moods, responds inappropriately to changing circumstances. Though Congress may be able to act upon foreign policy, in George Kennan's words, "fitfully, in great ponderous lurches,"[26] astute adjustments to changing circumstances are beyond the compass of congressional wisdom and ability. Consequently, if the difficult and sensitive challenges of international relations are to be met, foreign policy should not come within the legislature's embrace.

In the eyes of many realists, a shortcoming compounding democracy's sluggishness resides in its excessive reluctance to use force, even when this is what circumstances call for. The values on which liberal democracy is founded and the practice of negotiating differences that is the hallmark of its political culture do not lead to easy belief in the virtues of military coercion. As Stanley Hoffmann has explained, "A liberal view of international affairs suffers from a complete misunderstanding of the role of force in world history. . . . Consequently, there still remains an instinctive inhibition in America's approach to the use of national force."[27]

Similarly, Samuel Huntington and Zbigniew Brzezinski (both sharing a fundamental belief in the role of power in international affairs) have contrasted U.S. reticence to use military tools with the lack of scruples displayed by Soviet leaders in this regard.[28] Though not everyone would agree that the United States has been especially reluctant to use coercion abroad, it is often claimed that American public attitudes toward armed force make it harder for the United States than for its rivals to use military instruments when conditions so require, decreasing the range of foreign policy tools that can be applied to external challenges.

If, because of disruptions from below, democratic foreign policy is ill-suited for timely responses to foreign threats, if it cannot optimally calibrate its behavior to changing external circumstances, if it is inconsistent and unwilling to resort to force when necessary, then plainly there is cause for concern. But not everyone agrees with this assessment of the democratic plight or of the dangers of disruption from below, and those who most vocally disagree are rarely enthusiastic advocates of realpolitik.

Many of the founding fathers were convinced of democracy's advantages for foreign as well as domestic affairs.[29] In this regard, as in many others, they were influenced by the ideas of the French Enlightenment, especially by the arguments of the *philosophes* against foreign policies founded on balance of power and diplomatic intrigue and for a diplomacy rooted in the Enlightenment notion of the "rule of reason." This, the French philosophers believed, would have to stem from a reorganized domestic political order involving popular control over the conduct of external policy (e.g., by ensuring legislative control over international treaties). Condorcet, for example, argued that ordinary people (the masses about which Morgenthau and Lippmann expressed such misgivings), unlike absolute monarchs, would always be peace-loving and that obstacles to the direct expression of popular will should be removed whenever possible in the interests of the international order.[30]

Moreover, and even at first glance, the historical record does not compellingly argue against popular control of foreign affairs. Writing in 1920, Lord James Bryce pointed out that there were three major instances in recent British history when the public disagreed with its government's foreign policy: the American Civil War, the Russo-Turkish friction of the late 1870s, and the Boer War. On each of these occasions the public's view was ultimately vindicated. By contrast, he noted that Russia, Germany, and Austria-Hungary had experienced major foreign policy disasters, even though these were countries in which "no popular clamour disturbed the Olympian heights where sat the monarch and his group of military and civilian advisers, controlling foreign policy as respects both ends and means."[31] Closer to home, it could be observed that the American public realized U.S. involvement in Vietnam was a mistake well before its government could bring itself to pull out of that divisive conflict.

It seems, then, that a plausible case could be made on both sides of the argument and that, despite the claims of realpolitik, our understanding does not reach beyond somewhat vague points and counterpoints. The empirical and analytical base on which judgments of disruption from below rests is thin and impressionistic; both the evidence and the standards of judgment must be taken further than has thus far been the case.

Derailment from Above

If disruption from below is an issue often entwined with the themes of realpolitik, the matter of derailment from above cannot as readily be linked to an established doctrine on international politics. Authors within the realist tradition do occasionally lament the foreign policy consequences of the way power is pursued and structured at the system's pinnacle. George Kennan, for example, has complained that "the evidence of one great failure or folly of American statesmanship has seemed never to have been brought into association with the way in which this country was constituted for the conduct of foreign policy in the first place."[32]

Where realists address the matter of derailment from above, they most often do so in a manner that makes their qualms intersect with concerns about disruption from below; for example, by complaining that too much authority is vested in the legislative branch, which, in turn, reflects the irrationality of the masses by which it is elected. However, not everyone views responsiveness to popular preference as a cross that democratic foreign policy must bear. In one instance a realist has even considered such responsiveness a substantial boon to international aspirations. Although Max Weber is best known as a political sociologist, key strands of his thinking identify him as a believer in realpolitik as well.[33]

More than a century after the *philosophes*, Weber argued the foreign policy virtues of democracy along different lines, invoking the need to cater to public opinion's beneficial impact on the quality of leadership. Although liberal in many respects, he was also a fervent nationalist who lamented that Germany's international position had fallen short of what he judged the superiority of its culture and its national mission merited.[34] In his view, much of the fault derived from the stranglehold that the Prussian and Junker oligarchy had imposed on government and from the bureaucratic and authoritarian structure of political power in Wilhelminian Germany. Together they promoted the stagnation of political and economic life, impeding vigorous growth and the dynamic policies that a successful empire required. What Germany most needed was charismatic leadership, closer to the sort that Britain managed to produce than to the ossified bureaucracies dominating German political life. The relevance for our purposes is that in Weber's estimate only a parliamentary democracy, preferably with a strong plebiscitary component, could produce the charismatic leaders capable of winning for Germany her rightful place in global society, for only under such conditions would leaders need to rouse popular enthusiasm and subject their own performance to ongoing popular scrutiny.

Thus, contrary to the views of many realists, it might be assumed that the quality of political leadership improves in rough proportion to the rigors of political competition for public support—something in which democracies plainly have the upper hand. If credible, the hypothesis may have special relevance for the United States where, according to one line of argument, the presidency itself has become a permanent struggle for mass approval: in a sense, a "plebiscitary presidency,"[35] in which the popular support enjoyed by a president at any moment is a measure of his ability to bring other politically potent actors behind his policy.[36]

Whether or not Weber's view is wellfounded is largely an empirical matter, to be more comprehensively addressed in chapter 4. The issue of leadership is, nonetheless, one upon which realists differ. In a vein akin to Weber's, Henry Kissinger, both an exponent and practitioner of realpolitik, expressed his disdain for the cautious and lumbering spirit of foreign policy bureaucrats, contrasting it to the vision and dynamism of strong and charismatic leaders.[37] Without explicitly identifying charisma with democratic competition for political power, he does not expect to find it within the ranks of governmental institutions—declaring, in the work that most closely defines his mindset, that "inspiration is a call for greatness; organization a recognition that mediocrity is the usual pattern of leadership."[38]

Weber's views stand in sharp contrast to those of George Kennan, who has shown little enthusiasm for foreign policy born of the rough and tumble of domestic politics, criticizing the tendency for "American diplomacy to degenerate into a series of postures struck before the American political audience, with only secondary consideration being given to the impact of these postures on our relations with other countries."[39]

In Kennan's opinion the most capable trustees of any nation's international interests are its professional diplomats (the bureaucrats about whom Kissinger expressed such qualms). Well-trained, dispassionate, with no personal political agenda, they are most likely to rise above parochial concerns and emotional drives and coolly guide foreign affairs on a course consistent with the national interest and the compulsions of global society.

If realists do not always concur on the category of leadership best suited to conduct external affairs, they generally do agree that foreign policy is the business of an elite insulated from popular pressures. While this follows from their misgivings about disruption from below, the assumption that, left to themselves, government leaders would conduct external affairs in a wise and effective manner is not unassailable, and concern with pressures originating within the body of society need not logically lead to a belief in the foreign-policy sagacity of those who stand above it.

Most evidently, one could argue that professional statesmen are not only apt to be swayed by popular emotions but are also capable of fanning them when this suits their purpose. Public beliefs find their reflection, often in amplified form, in the utterances of political leaders, and political sobriety has been undermined by impulses manifested at their level as well. One could further claim that U.S. politicians, including presidents and presidential aspirants, frequently shape their foreign policy positions around their short-term political (especially electoral) ambitions, further undermining prospects that foreign policy would be based on sober realpolitik.

The proposition that officials of foreign policy bureaucracies will do much better is also open to debate, for it could be argued that they rarely manage to escape the operating routines, concern with narrow organizational interests, and perceptual blinders associated with roles in complex governmental institutions.[40] If this characterization is accepted, increased faith in bureaucracy is not a credible redress for whatever foreign policy shortcomings the nation may display.

While the problems referred to above are largely behavioral, derailment from above may also include a structural dimension. The incohesiveness and lack of continuity in U.S. foreign policy have been blamed, not just on the incentives by which national leaders are guided, but on the manner in which authority is structured at the political system's pinnacle—in particular, on the institutional pluralism that defines democratic control in the United States. One problem even in nonrealist eyes is that the need to produce a consensus may become more important than the external circumstances to which foreign policy is the apparent response. According to Theodore Lowi the difficulty of achieving consensus in the face of such diversity impels leadership to overstate challenges and oversell solutions,[41] making American democracy, in Macaulay's words, "all sail and no anchor."[42]

Though pluralism has manifold expressions, one that directly reflects the founding fathers' design is the principle of separated yet shared powers that, in foreign affairs, is reflected in the joint allocation of policy authority to the executive and to the legislative branch of government. In fact, in terms of explicit grants of constitutional authority in this area, Congress has fared better than the executive branch—an aspect of U.S. democracy often perplexing to foreign observers.[43] Joseph Nye has observed that the congressional-executive division of foreign policy power "not only contributes to incoherence" but also to a situation where "the executive must simplify and exaggerate to overcome the inertia of a diverse and loosely structured body of 535 individuals with weak party loyalties."[44] The result, once again, is that foreign policy may be more intemperate than warranted by international conditions.

Although the suitability of bifurcated institutional authority for the conduct of international affairs is often questioned, it could also be that policy informed by the judgment and expertise of two branches of government stands to be wiser than where either branch of government can too easily subdue the other. Accordingly, many might agree with Kenneth Waltz that "American institutions facilitate rather than discourage the quick identification of problems, the pragmatic quest for solutions, the ready confrontation of dangers, the willing expenditure of energies, and the open criticism of policies."[45]

The more closely one looks the more it appears that plausible cases can be argued on both sides of the theme of derailment from above, and there is little of a prima facie nature to help select among parallel but opposite claims. Two further points must be made at this juncture.

The first is that while political realists see a good deal of conflict between democratic political involvement and foreign policy, those who hold more benign views on the nature of international relations are less likely to perceive such friction. We have already had an indication of this with Condorcet, but the best illustration is provided by authors falling under the loosely-defined rubric of idealists. Without neglecting the diversity of opinion within this school, idealists do share a number of key beliefs. Confident in the perfectibility of human nature, they reject notions of insatiable national power drives and security dilemmas, maintaining that more constructive impulses spring from the sagacity of public opinion than from the assumptions that guide practicing politicians. Accordingly, they are more likely to welcome than to lament pressures on foreign policy from the body of society. The surge of authors and activists pressing for collective security by appealing directly to popular opinion in the wake of World War I furnished a powerful statement of the idealist credo.[46]

Even those who neither believe in peace through human perfectibility or in the hard-nosed assumptions of realpolitik are generally tolerant of those aspects of democracy that realists most often complain about. In this regard, it is worth contrasting Jimmy Carter, who came to office seeking to replace the quest for Cold War advantage with the international promotion of human rights, and who invited congressional involvement in international affairs, with Richard Nixon and Henry Kissinger, firm political realists who held to unfettered executive supremacy in matters of foreign policy.

The Reciprocal Perspective

The consequences for foreign policy of internal political conditions are linked by a feedback loop to the consequences of external affairs for domestic political norms and practices. This may seem obvious as a general principle but it has particular bearing on the United States. While few nations fully escape the domestic repercussions of external events, two types of countries experience their influence most deeply—those that are very weak and those that are very strong. It is not surprising that small or powerless nations should find themselves easily penetrated from without and buffeted by external pressures that escape their control. It is less apparent why powerful states do not more successfully insulate their domestic affairs from international currents but the explanation emerges upon reflection. Countries that can mold the course of international events are often led to equate their national interest, and by extension their domestic needs, with an ambitious and understandably self-centered vision of the international order. Because an a priori link is established between external and internal goals, and because such nations are in a position to act on this link, foreign policy reverberates domestically, often touching the foundations upon which the political order is established.

This is compounded by the extent to which various actors in the domestic political arena seek to influence external priorities. Even the categories of international goals that are common to most nations have a content that specifically reflects each society's prevailing pattern of interests and beliefs. They may be aggregated in a more or less democratic manner but it would be wrong to assume that any country's foreign policy objectives are entirely divorced from the parochial weal. Interbureaucratic struggles for authority and shares of the budgetary pie, economic actors' pursuit of gain, the preferences of ethnic groups and other narrow interests, comprise the vectors of which foreign policy is, in most cases, the resultant. The greater is a nation's ability to act internationally, the more numerous and forceful will be the domestic forces seeking to mold its foreign policy. In turn, their preferences and interests are shaped and reshaped through the process of formulating and implementing foreign policy. "Created by wars that required it, the machine now created the wars it required," Joseph Schumpeter observed with respect to the military elite of ancient Egypt, capturing a more general reciprocal relationship between sociopolitical structure and foreign policy.[47]

A decision to rely on military instruments rather than, say, economic pressure to alter another country's behavior may affect the structure of domestic preferences and power by improving the position of the military establishment and its supporters and, conceivably, of those trading interests that might have borne the reverse consequences of economic warfare. Moreover, the repercussions of foreign policy successes and failures also tend to be reflected domestically. For instance, sectors of the economy seeking protection from foreign competition will be either fortified or weakened depending on whether the protectionist policies do or do not manage to repel competition; and successful military action abroad may strengthen belief in the virtues of coercion, bolstering support for the nation's armed forces.

More specifically yet, a government charged with designing and implementing foreign policies must marshal that society's human and material resources toward this end. The support of those groups on whose shoulders the burdens of policy rest most heavily must be secured, and domestic and international priorities, occasionally even political institutions and practices, may have to be adjusted to ensure that this backing is acquired. Part of this logic is that foreign policy decision-makers must be manipulators of domestic politics, and the more ambitious the external goals, the more likely it is that their pursuit will leave domestic traces.

Consequently, the conduct of foreign policy affects the domestic societal sources from which it flows and, by extension, the political matrix in which these sources are embedded. And, whatever the influences that force domestic politics into the mold of external concerns, their effect is amplified by dominant beliefs about the consequences of the free play of democratic practices for the country's foreign policy. Because of this, a conviction that effective foreign policy and liberal democracy are fundamentally incompatible generally leads to compromises on domestic political principles. Thus, the effects of foreign policy ripple through the political fabric, and, in the American case, this has stimulated at least two sorts of qualms: a fear of executive hegemony and concern about insufficient governmental candor.

Executive Hegemony It is sometimes lamented that, as a result of America's expanding international role, the presidency and the executive branch of government have appropriated a foreign policy role far beyond what the Constitution intended—jolting the relation between branches of government out of its proper equilibrium and undermining a pillar of U.S. democratic doctrine and practice.

Never have these apprehensions been as insistently voiced as during the presidency of Richard M. Nixon, when warnings of an "imperial presidency" were often heard,[48] and whose consequences were said to include "the all-purpose invocation of 'national security,' the insistence on executive secrecy, the withholding of information from Congress, the refusal to spend funds appropriated by Congress, the attempted intimidation of the press, [and] the use of the White House itself as a base for espionage and sabotage directed against the political opposition."[49]

The sources of this concern were understandable. Nixon was rarely far from arguing that the ends justified the means, and that these means could involve departures from accepted democratic tenets. As he explained in his memoirs, "I felt that we were at a historical turning point. My reading of history taught that when all the leadership institutions of a nation become paralyzed with self-doubt and second thoughts, that nation cannot long survive unless those institutions are either reformed, replaced, or circumvented. In my second term I was prepared to adopt whichever of these three methods—or whichever combination of them—was necessary."[50]

One could argue that the executive appropriation of powers vested elsewhere by the Constitution was an ephemeral phenomenon associated with a brief chapter of U.S. postwar history, and that comparable excesses have not been witnessed before or since. Still, worries may linger. To begin with, the Nixon interlude highlights the range of the possible in political life, especially when international necessity is invoked to justify departures from normal democratic practices. Secondly, and in several less dramatic ways, the relation between branches of government may indeed have slipped out of its constitutionally mandated balance.

Few decisions affect a nation's fate as much as those regarding war and peace, and democracy's meaning would be much shallower if such matters escaped popular control. The Constitution grants Congress the sole power to "declare war," while designating the president commander in chief of the armed forces, responsible for the operational conduct of hostilities once they have occurred. Nevertheless, the vast majority of America's military engagements, both brief police actions and protracted wars, have not been pursuant to Congressional decision and, by bending the definition of war and reinterpreting the meaning of the commander in chief designation, U.S. presidents may have appropriated a function that both democratic theory and original intent had granted Congress.

Presidents may also have overstepped their constitutional and democratic prerogatives with regard to treaty commitments. The Constitution empowers the president to make treaties but provides that this must be done with the "advice and consent" of the Senate. As treaties are a source of domestic law, it is natural that the legislative branch should have a role in the matter, and the Senate is called upon to decide, by a two-thirds majority, whether to authorize their ratification. Yet, here too, it could be argued that presidential power has displaced congressional authority, as the vast majority of foreign commitments are undertaken through executive agreements rather than formal treaties. The volume of international business conducted by a superpower makes it inconceivable that all, or even most, obligations contracted abroad should be subject to parliamentary authorization. But under the circumstances a pillar of democratic control may simply be incompatible with external ambitions of a certain scope.

Governmental Candor   There are other ways in which foreign policy may grind at the cornerstones of American democracy. Political accountability logically assumes that the public, directly or through its immediate representatives, can find out what its government is doing, and the openness with which policy is conducted is a major standard of democratic performance. Still, openness can never be an absolute principle, and there are circumstances that may justify curtailing freedom of information, no matter how highly political accountability is valued in principle. The concern is that once secrecy and deception wrest acceptability from a society their cloak may be stretched to cover governmental incompetence, misuses of power, and other shady practices—allowing them to escape popular control and censure.

But the concern's normative and empirical foundation cannot be easily evaluated. Unlike Great Britain, for example, the United States does not have an Official Secrets Act, and it could be reasoned that the Freedom of Information Act makes it hard for the government to withhold information without demonstrating a compelling need for secrecy. At the same time, a government absorbed with security and far-flung international goals may not be able to resist feeling, more often than can be justified, that it is in the public's interest to know less rather than more. As a former chairman of the Joint Chiefs of Staff, General Maxwell Taylor, explained in response to a question about the public's right to know: "I don't believe in it as a general principle. . . . A citizen should know those things he needs to know to be a good citizen and discharge his functions."[51]

Obviously, such beliefs on governmental candor do not spring from an intellectual vacuum; they are, explicitly or implicitly rooted in two of the assumptions at the heart of realpolitik: (1) that in a potentially hostile world, where national survival depends on the proper management of power, domestic political principle must not interfere with the primacy of foreign policy, and (2) that the public and its representatives cannot be expected to respond sensibly to vital policy information—making domestically directed secrecy and prevarication the lesser of two evils.

More direct concerns about democratic rights have been raised. The gravest assaults on individual liberties were associated with America's crusade against Communism and justified by the threat of foreign subversion. In stunned reaction to the Bolshevik Revolution the government clamped down on the leftist Industrial Workers of the World (IWW) trade union in 1917, and Attorney General A. Mitchell Palmer jailed thousands of suspected "alien subversives." The postwar prosecutions of members of the American Communist Party (based on the Smith Act of 1940), the investigation of Hollywood screenwriters by the House Committee on Un-American Activities for alleged Communist associations, and the excesses of Senator Joseph R. McCarthy, were more recent expressions of the domestic consequences of intense security fears. While the paranoia of the 1950s has not been apparent in subsequent decades, it demonstrated that individual liberties may be considered dispensable in a nation besieged by international apprehensions and the specter of foreign rivals. "Perhaps it is a universal truth," James Madison once remarked, "that the loss of liberty at home is to be charged to provisions against danger, real or pretended, from abroad."[52]

Nevertheless, the starting point at which democratic liberties become vulnerable to abuses justified by external necessity may be precisely that point at which governmental openness comes to be considered dispensable. Even if political closure need not be the proximate cause of other abuses, it is, as Edward Shils has often argued, their harbinger.[53] Consequently, the impact of external pursuits on governmental candor, and the extent to which there may be a natural friction between the two, is an important issue in the study of democracy and foreign policy. One facet of the matter is to decide what harm, if any, political candor may do to the nation's international interests. The other is to decide when compromises to the principle of political openness outweigh the danger of staunchly adhering to it—a judgment that must rest on a more thorough examination of the assumptions underlying the presumed trade-off between democracy and foreign policy.

An Outline of the Argument

The purpose of the preceding survey of opinions, claims, and counterclaims has been to highlight the range of plausible views in this area. From the muddle two important points emerge. The first is that friction between democracy and foreign policy can, in principle, have two sources: disruption from below and/or derailment from above. Both have consequences for the quality of foreign policy, but they rest on distinct assumptions, and their implications for domestic political practice are quite different. The second point is that the consequences of democracy for foreign policy are entwined with the consequences of external policy for democracy—making it necessary to discuss each in the other's light. In particular, and given its many domestic ramifications, it is useful to examine the need for, and the implications of, governmental deception of its own public for foreign policy ends.

The book will argue that there may be some trade-off between democracy and the wisdom and effectiveness of U.S. foreign policy— but not for the reasons given by most political realists. Neither public pressures nor congressional involvement need make U.S. foreign relations any worse (or, for that matter, significantly better) than would be the case under conditions of greater executive autonomy. The problem, if any, revolves around the pattern of incentives created by a liberal democracy at the pinnacle of the political system.

The dense tangle of claims and refutations on such issues make it difficult to tread on entirely virgin territory. Nevertheless, much that will be said deviates from dominant opinion. The thesis of disruption from below is not, as we have seen, universally accepted, but it is certainly the ruling perspective. By rejecting it, I am rejecting much of the literature on democracy and foreign policy. Moreover, if the clash between electoral political competition and effective foreign policy is sometimes alluded to, the benefits of competition are far more frequently addressed than its liabilities. In other words, as the first part of the book will argue, the components of a criticism of democracy's foreign policy implications are frequently misplaced.

The corollary theme is that, to a greater extent than is usually recognized, the goals and methods of U.S. foreign policy are not neutral with respect to the domestic norms that Americans wish to live by. Much as there may be a point beyond which the scope and intensity of external interests start sapping the economic bases of a country's power, so there may be a threshold beyond which international ambitions, and the methods by which they are pursued, begin lapping at the foundations of domestic political principle—a problem magnified by misguided assumptions about the sources of conflict between political principle and effective policy.

This book focuses on questions with empirical answers, but such answers are sometimes insufficient. In particular, any discussion of the link between domestic political conditions and the quality of foreign policy must involve some notion of the criteria by which desirable policy is defined. Though most such standards may be inherently tenuous (an argument further developed in chapter 6), it is useful, at least as a point of departure, to assume that there is an objective and knowable measure of good foreign policy. In settling on appropriate criteria, we can proceed in two ways: (1) by adopting the standards of political realism, the dominant doctrine of contemporary international relations theory, or (2) by seeking to transcend the criteria of realpolitik.

Since so much of the critique of democracy's impact on international affairs flows from the pens of realists, we may begin, if only for purposes of argument, by adopting their view of good foreign policy. No single characterization would satisfy the conception of every author writing in that tradition, but, taken together, three rules go far toward characterizing a good foreign policy from the realpolitik perspective.[54]

The first of the three is that policy should not confuse ideals, desired essentially for their emotional or ethical appeal, with interests, desired for their pragmatic benefits to the state or nation. Ethical ideals have a role in domestic affairs, as they most certainly do in personal pursuits, but in the view of most political realists they have no useful function in the harsh world of international power strug-

gles. There is no room for moralism, legalism, or any value whose
attraction, in an international context, is primarily emotional. The
second rule is that interests and power should be brought into proper
balance: never reaching for more than one's power allows, while
always seeking to acquire the power needed to attain one's external
aspirations. The third rule is that the actual conduct of foreign affairs
should proceed in a measured, consistent fashion; volatile and in-
constant responses to the outside world or any behavior that departs
from the norms of prudence would collide with the dictates of political realism.

These three rules summarize the prescriptive core of realpolitik
and define many concerns about the compatibility of democracy and
foreign policy, but they need not be taken at face value; the quality
of policy can also be judged by broader criteria. This applies particularly to the first of the three, for, while no one would seriously
suggest that aspiration should outrun power or that policy should
be imprudently conducted, the notion that interests may not be defined in terms of loftier principles is debatable. To begin with, a
society is presumably entitled to define its interests in terms of its
own values, and if some of them have an ethical or moral tone, this
does not mean that their pursuit cannot have the status of interests
from that society's perspective. It could be further argued that power,
defined as the ability to influence the conduct of other nations, depends on moral authority as well as on coercive ability; if so, an
effective foreign policy should be associated with some objectives that
are likely to have broad international appeal.

Thus, in evaluating the foreign policy consequences of U.S. democracy, one may choose to abide by the criteria of realpolitik or to
reach beyond them. In the first case, we could ask two sorts of questions: (1) whether democracy does indeed exhibit the traits that realism so claims, and (2) whether these democratic properties do indeed
impair the conduct of foreign policy according to realist precepts. It
is at least logically possible that a positive answer to the first question
would not imply an affirmative response to the second one; similarly,
if U.S. democracy does display characteristics that are incompatible
with realpolitik, these same failings might also preclude the successful
pursuit of goals permeated with more of an idealist content. But it
is also possible that the same conclusions about democracy would
not be reached if we chose a different standard of successful foreign

policy. In other words, what might stand in the way of attaining one conception of a desirable foreign policy, might promote (or at least be neutral with regard to) the attainment of another conception. Accordingly, the book will begin by relying on the general standards of realpolitik, while subsequently considering whether other criteria for a good foreign policy might not be equally or more valid. It will also (in chapter 6) discuss the feasibility of devising *any* generally valid definition of the national interest, and the possible implications of an inability to do so.

In summary, this book addresses a number of assumptions, some of which have attained the status of conventional wisdom, on the consequences of democracy for foreign policy. Several things, however, do not come within its ambit. To begin with, it does not deal with the relation between democracy and foreign policy in comparative perspective. This is certainly worth doing, and doubtless it will be done by others, but my concern is with that relation as it applies to the United States. The substantive importance of the American case, even from the broader international perspective, should justify the enterprise in its own right. Secondly, I carry no particular methodological brief. As far as is within my ability, I have adapted the technique of inquiry to the nature of the question being asked. Consequently, the approach ranges from quantitative and statistical, when this is appropriate, to historical and analytical, when a closer focus is called for. Inevitably, some will feel that their own approach is not done proper justice, and within their own terms of reference they may be right. However, the reciprocal effects of American democracy and U.S. foreign policy raise a variety of questions that cannot be adequately addressed within the terms of a single methodological credo. A complex subject requires a multilayered approach.

Like most books this one is an incomplete enterprise. For example, it focuses on popular sentiment and governmental institutions, while having less to say about interest groups or other informal sources of power. The justifications rest on the usual limitations of any scholarly endeavor; still, I feel that the issues discussed in this volume cover much that is essential about the relationship between democracy and foreign policy in the United States.

Chapter 2

THE MENTALITY
OF THE MASSES

*Not all persons in leadership echelons have pre-
cisely the same basic beliefs; some may even
regard the people as a beast.* —V. O. Key

The main pillar on which the theme of disruption from below rests
is its unflattering conception of the popular mind. Political realists,
moreover, are not alone in the low esteem in which they hold mass
opinion; indeed, this is the dominant sentiment of those who count
a successful foreign policy among their leading concerns. Accordingly, an ability to insulate policy from popular sentiment, or to
actively mold the latter in conformity with the statesman's conception of realpolitik, are often deemed the mark of capable leadership.
In his study of State Department officials, for example, Bernard Cohen
revealed that they felt the American public had very little to contribute to a wise foreign policy.[1] Like Morgenthau, Zbigniew Brzezinski has urged a manipulatory rather than reactive approach to
public opinion, arguing that the president "needs to be an effective
mobilizer of political support, a persuasive educator who simultaneously enlightens the public about global complexities and generates
support for his policies."[2]

   This disinclination to indulge the popular mind is rooted in two
of its assumed properties: (1) its shallow understanding of the issues,

and (2) the unstructured, and correspondingly volatile, character of the sentiments it chooses to express. As the public neither knows nor cares much about external events, there is no point in submitting complex and important international matters to its judgment. If additionally—both for reasons of temperament and inadequate information—popular sentiment is at times lethargic and can be stirred to action only by major shocks, while it yields at other times to irrational emotion, a readiness to follow its dictates might imply irresponsible statesmanship.

Those who fear that realpolitik and an attentiveness to public sentiment are largely incompatible can draw no comfort from the U.S. government's responsiveness to popular pressure. While this sensitivity is sometimes assumed to be a recent phenomenon, linked in part to the ability of the electronic media to instantly diffuse information about governmental policies and pronouncements, the tradition has a considerable place in American history. It is worth remembering that the two most momentous foreign policy statements of the nation's first half-century—the Farewell Address and the Monroe Doctrine—were directed primarily to the American people, not to foreign nations. In any case, while government may mold and manipulate public perceptions of international affairs, it is also very attentive to what it perceives public sentiment to be. Such, in any case, is the nearly unanimous judgment of the empirical research devoted to the matter.

A study conducted in the early 1970s comparing public preferences revealed by polling data on several national issues with actual policies concluded that the extent of congruence on foreign policy matters was roughly comparable to that encountered for domestic issues.[3] Another study found that the correlation between public opinion and government policy was even more pronounced in the case of foreign policy (a 92 percent congruence between public opinion on twenty-four issues of foreign policy and policy outcomes.)[4] Both studies sought only to establish whether opinions and policies overlapped. Since each left open the question of causal direction, their findings are as consistent with the hypothesis that the public tends to identify (spontaneously or through manipulation) with whatever it is that the government happens to be doing as with the hypothesis that the government takes its cues from the public.

More recent research has addressed the question of causal direction by comparing policy changes with opinion shifts at various points in time, to see which preceded which. Again, a pattern of consistency between policy and public sentiment was found, especially for issues that are central to the public's concern and on which its opinions are fairly well defined.[5] Overall, a slightly stronger coincidence between opinion and policy was found for domestic (70 percent of the cases) than for foreign (62 percent of the cases) issues. Just as importantly, in the majority of cases opinion shifted *before* policy changed, suggesting that the former usually engendered the latter. Although this was true in only slightly more than half the cases, the authors pointed out that instances of incongruence were often found on the less visible and less politically salient issues. In a similar vein, Bruce Russett has inquired whether governmental decisions on levels of military spending followed or preceded shifting public views on whether increases were necessary. He found that the statistically strongest relation was between public opinion in a given year and changes in actual spending in the subsequent year.[6]

More research may be needed before definitive answers to the question of governmental responsiveness can be given, but that which is available suggests a fair amount of sensitivity to popular preference in foreign as well as domestic policy. Under the circumstances, and given the qualms of realpolitik, the question is whether this responsiveness has welcome or undesirable consequences for U.S. foreign policy.

This chapter will argue that, while the qualms of realists are overstated, judgments must depend on the *type* of views one assumes popular opinion to encompass (for example, are we referring to the public's cognitions or desires?). As a first step, however, we must ask the essentially descriptive question of whether popular opinion does in fact approximate the portrait offered by those who worry most about disruption from below. Following the descriptive survey, we will undertake the analytically more constructive task of examining the *kinds* of awareness required of the U.S. public if foreign policy is not to suffer from its influence.

A Vapid and Ill-informed Public

On the whole, it has been easy to portray the American public as one knowing little about major political issues and not eager to learn more. The key to this portrayal is provided by absolute figures regarding the factual knowledge possessed by the average American on fairly specific issues of politics and policy. In 1955 and again in 1970 nearly 40 percent of all Americans were unaware that U.S. presidents are limited to two terms in office.[7] In 1973 no more than 50 percent of all adult Americans knew who their congressman was. In 1975 just over one third of the respondents in a national survey could identify both of their home state U.S. senators; in the same poll, one quarter of those surveyed either had never heard of, or knew very little about, Gerald Ford, the incumbent president.[8] These figures depict a public with scant understanding of, or interest in, the political process, and the situation appears no better when we turn to international affairs.

Although U.S. military involvement in Vietnam lasted eight years, cost the nation 58,000 lives, and generated more domestic unrest than the United States had witnessed since the Civil War, less than two thirds of the public knew, in 1985, that the United States had supported South Vietnam in that war.[9] In the early 1980s the administration portrayed Central America as a crucial arena of the East-West struggle, and events in the region were regularly covered by the media. Although the United States provided significant aid to Napoleon Duarte's moderate government in El Salvador and, amid great domestic controversy, launched an effort, mainly through military support of the Contra insurgents, to remove the leftist Sandinista government from power in Nicaragua, only 32 percent of the respondents in a 1984 survey knew that El Salvador was a nation with which the United States had friendly relations, while 56 percent thought that the Contra rebels in Nicaragua were either enemies or not friendly to the United States.[10]

Other examples of apparent public ignorance can be found as well. A survey taken in 1964 revealed that only 58 percent of the public knew that the United States belonged to NATO, while 38 percent thought that the Soviet Union was a member.[11] In a similar vein, in 1988 fifty percent of all respondents could not name *any* members of the Warsaw Pact.[12] During the 1970s the SALT negotiations were the main focus of U.S.-Soviet relations and they were the object of a lively domestic debate; yet in a 1979 poll only 34 percent of the public could correctly identify the two nations involved in the negotiations. When this was done for them, only 58 percent knew that the talks concerned long-range weapons, 27 percent had no idea what they dealt with, and the remainder was about equally divided among those who thought the talks dealt with troop reductions in Europe, U.S.-Soviet trade, and limiting arms sales to the Third World.[13]

Obviously, these statistics do not portray the public in a flattering light; and they lend support to the notion that, in important matters of state, not too much weight should be given opinions resting on so slim a foundation of factual knowledge. Still, none of this is truly surprising. U.S. citizens, as those of most democracies, are not primarily political animals. More than a century and a half ago, Alexis de Tocqueville pointed out that Americans were much more concerned with private and material pursuits than with matters of broad public interest or with philosophical questions—an assessment that seems substantially accurate today as well.[14]

The U.S. public is not alone in its political indifference. Certain democracies register even lower levels of voter turnout than does the United States. Though others show greater citizen participation in elections, this is often achieved by making voting mandatory and by fining those who do not appear at the booth on election day.[15] The problem of political apathy has long historical roots: despite its vaunted commitment to citizen participation in public affairs, Athenian democracy at the time of Pericles seems to have had difficulties stirring up sufficient public interest to obtain a quorum in the Athenian Assembly. In fact, it is reported that "to ensure adequate attendance at a dull Assembly meeting, police with long ropes dipped in wet paint herded citizens to Pnyx Hill," where the assembly convened.[16]

A variety of theories have sought to account for the pattern of personal interests that we see around us, but the dominant view is that issues of general national policy appear too distant from the concerns of a people seeking fulfillment mainly in private life and material gratification. Moreover, one would expect this distance to seem especially great with regard to foreign affairs, where the consequences of governmental action for personal interests are less directly apparent than in the case of domestic policy. Foreign aid to Africa, aid to Contra rebels in Nicaragua, and negotiations with the Soviet Union on conventional force reductions in Europe are issues that most people find hard to connect to their immediate concerns. Accordingly, when Americans are moved by national problems, these are more likely to involve domestic than foreign policy. In particular, the U.S. public is stirred by economic matters. When asked to identify what, in their opinion, constitutes the major national problem, well over half of the respondents typically select "pocketbook" issues, while far fewer choose foreign affairs. In 1980—a year marked by such events as the Soviet invasion of Afghanistan and the plight of the U.S. hostages in Iran—only 44 percent of the public said that foreign policy problems worried them most, while 43 percent chose inflation or unemployment. And that was probably a high-water mark in public concern with international affairs. In a more typical year between 10 and 20 percent of the public say they are most worried about some international problem while 60 to 70 percent place economic issues at the top of their list of concerns.[17]

However, the public is not an undifferentiated entity and some of its segments know and care more about foreign policy than others. An early and still very useful model of the U.S. public, offered by James Rosenau, depicted it as a pyramid with three levels.[18] At its apex is the tier of *opinion makers*, including prominent journalists, professors, business executives, and the like. Because this elite by virtue of its knowledge and influence is in a position to mold the views of others, its opinions are taken quite seriously by those who are in a position to make actual foreign policy decisions. It constitutes, however, a very small fraction of the public. At the pyramid's base is the *mass public*; in its middle section the *attentive public*. According to this model, the mass public comprises between 75 and 90 percent of the adult population. By and large, it knows virtually nothing about foreign policy and does not care to know much more. The mass public's response to issues is "less one of intellect and more one of emotion, less one of opinion and more one of mood." And while the dominant mood is "indifference and passivity," it occasionally swings from one extreme to another—from tolerance to intolerance, idealism to cynicism, withdrawal to interventionism. The attentive public, on the other hand, is reasonably knowledgeable and cares more about international affairs; its opinions show "greater structure and depth." Because it is relatively sophisticated, the attentive public "tends to offset the irrational impact of mass moods and to fill the vacuum that exists when indifference is the prevailing mood." It is therefore a moderating influence that compels a measure of governmental accountability in the conduct of foreign relations. Still, its ranks are quite limited: between one-tenth and one quarter of the population, and the vast majority of Americans belong to the mass public.

In recognizing that the U.S. public is not homogenous in its information about or interest in foreign policy, while concluding that by far its largest segment knows and cares little about external affairs, Rosenau's three-tiered model of public opinion corresponds to the conceptions of a variety of other authors.[19] If one assumes that authentic democracy requires popular input into crucial decisions, both at the voting booth and between elections, one might conclude that the public is in no position to participate in the process of democratic policymaking where foreign affairs are concerned. Even if democratic participation were defined more narrowly, merely as the business of expressing approval or disapproval of a government every several years at the ballot box, the same conclusion might be reached—for if voters do not grasp the basics of important foreign policy issues (e.g., what major international agreements are about or which parties the United States is backing in various regional conflicts) they are unlikely to know which policies should be rewarded or punished at election time.

It could be pointed out that the average citizen is not especially well informed about domestic affairs either, and that foreign policy knowledge does not, despite the assumption of different levels of public attentiveness to the two arenas, compare unfavorably. For example, in October 1987 the Gallup Poll reported that 54 percent of the public had heard about the Central American peace plan proposed by the presidents of five Latin American nations and designed to end the conflict in Nicaragua. The same survey established that, of the six leading candidates for the Democratic nomination, only one (Jesse Jackson) was recognized by a majority of Democrats or Democratic-leaning independents.[20]

Nevertheless, there is an important difference between *specific* issues of foreign and domestic policy, since there are usually fewer national constituencies that are directly affected by foreign than by domestic policy. In the case of, say, national educational or full-employment policy it is usually easy to identify groups whose interests are immediately involved (teachers and students, in the first example, unemployed workers, in the second). Since these interests create "natural" constituencies ("issue publics") for or against the policies, the link between public and policy is automatically established; those to whom the policy most matters are likely to have an informed opinion about it and to convey their feelings to the government. But it is less easy to identify groups whose interests are as directly affected by foreign policy decisions, and the average citizen generally fails to see a plausible link between personal interests and external relations; consequently, he or she is more likely to be indifferent to matters of foreign than domestic policy.

Bleak portrayals of the public mind go beyond criticisms of its relative ignorance to lament the incoherence and instability of the opinions it is inclined to express. At times, this implies that moods are too extreme and inflexible to serve as a guide to sensible policy. Often too, it suggests that mass sentiment drives policy toward inconsistent ends. Moreover, these callow opinions are subject to unexpected shifts, making it difficult to hold policy to the steady course required to create appropriate expectations on the part of other members of the international system. Does this conception of public opinion as "erratic" and "undependable"[21] correspond to what the data reveals?

A Moody and Volatile Public?

It is often recognized, as Lippmann argued, that the severe settlement imposed by the Allies on Germany after World War I contributed to the rabid nationalism associated with the Nazis' rise to power. The British public's determination to "squeeze the orange until the pips squeak," and the French insistence that "les boches paieront" allowed little flexibility in dealing with Germany after its defeat. Despite its initial bellicosity, several years later the citizenry of most Western democracies could not muster the will to challenge Hitler over Austria or Czechoslovakia. Neville Chamberlain's policy of appeasement flowed largely from his conviction that the British population had no appetite for a confrontation with Germany. Similarly, although a timely U.S. response to German and Italian aggression might have curtailed the war's scope and duration, it was precluded by U.S. public sentiment that ran overwhelmingly against intervention at the time (table 2.1).

By he end of World War II, however, the American public had shed its reticence about confronting foreign foes—as demonstrated

TABLE 2.1
*Percent Stating that the United States Should
Stay Out of the War with Germany and Italy*

Date	Should Stay Out
March 1938	83%
September 1939	84%
May 1940	86%
January 1941	88%
October 1941	79%

SOURCE: The Gallup Poll

by its feelings toward the Soviet Union. Indeed, the Truman administration's hard line toward Moscow in the late 1940s may have been encouraged by his realiziation that most Americans had come to believe the worst of their erstwhile ally. As Arthur Schlesinger, Jr., observed, "[It was] the mass of ordinary people who first became angry over Soviet actions and then turned the Truman administration around. . . . The driving force . . . has come not from the top but from below."[22]

According to many conservatives, however, the U.S. public slipped into a state of lethargy on Cold War issues several decades later, and simply would not face the hard decisions required to oppose their country's leading adversary. Many hawks fretted about the consequences of a complacent public mood. Norman Podhoretz lamented the "culture of appeasement," while Richard Perle, an assistant secretary of defense and long-time opponent of cooperation with Moscow explained that "democracies will not sacrifice to protect their security in the absence of a sense of danger. And every time we create the impression that we and the Soviets are cooperating and moderating the competition, we diminish that sense of apprehension."[23]

These examples suggests that a major problem with public sentiment may be its disposition to err on the side of either excessive passivity or explosive volatility, lurching between the two extremes and discouraging a consistent and measured foreign policy. If political leaders patiently waited for the public to recognize foreign challenges before undertaking appropriate action, the country's international position and security could be imperiled by tardy responses. If, on the other hand, they tailored policy to the excesses demanded by an aroused populace, ill-considered policies would be the result.

This may be termed the *chaotic/impulsive* model of public opinion. It has gained credence, not only because of its apparent corroboration by history, but also because volatility and incoherence of opinion seem inversely related to depth of information. Since Rosenau's mass public displays so shallow a foundation of knowledge, it is natural, according to him, that its response to international events should be "less one of intellect and more one of emotion, less one of opinion and more one of mood." And although the usual mood "is, of course, indifference and passivity," it sometimes "swings from one extreme to another."[24] This view of the popular mind is consistent with the thinking of other authors as well. Philip Converse, for example, noted in his study of mass belief systems that the public (as opposed to elites) exhibits very little "constraints" among its various opinions. Because these opinions are not mutually linked and anchored by a contextual grasp, they may be erratic and tenuously connected to reality.[25] Similarly, Johan Galtung has argued that knowledge and intellectual sophistication generate a relatively pragmatic approach to foreign affairs, wherein the need for frequent policy adjustments in response to objective changes in international circumstances is recognized, but where the magnitude of the desired changes will generally be moderate. This stability is largely due to the "anchoring influence of ideologies." Ideology being simply conceived of as a structured body of political thought, it is usually the property of a society's sociocultural and economic elites. By contrast, the shallower nature of mass awareness, which lacks the structure of a proper ideology, is conducive to responses that are both more erratic and more extreme.[26]

Thus, there are respectable intellectual grounds for assuming that mass opinions are guided by inchoate sentiment rather than by a firm grasp of events, therefore exhibiting the inconstancy that is frequently ascribed to them. Such a view apparently was held by Gouverneur Morris (one of the more elitist of the founding fathers), who cautioned the Constitutional Convention, "The mob begins to think and reason. Poor reptiles! . . . They bask in the sun, and ere noon they will bite, depend upon it."[27] Using comparably bestial imagery, George F. Kennan complained,

> Democracy is . . . similar to one of those prehistoric monsters with a body as long as this room and a brain the size of a pin: he lies there in his primeval mud and pays little attention to his en-

vironment: he is slow to wrath—in fact, you practically have to whack his tail off to make him aware that his interests are being disturbed; but once he grasps this, he lays about him with such blind determination that he not only destroys his adversary but largely wrecks his native habitat.[28]

This, then, is a major concern connected to disruption from below, and we must inquire how closely this image of the public fits observable reality. Have average Americans in recent years conformed to the image of a public slumbering when it should be alert—irrationally lashing out at real or imagined adversaries when aroused? Have their feelings been volatile and intemperate, lacking a grounding in objective circumstances and a coherent relation to each other? For the most part, these are empirical questions requiring that us to examine the evidence of public opinion on issues of particular foreign policy significance.

The East-West Struggle and National Security

During the past several decades, most of America's external anxieties and hopes, most of its animosities and friendships, have, directly or indirectly, stemmed from its rivalry with the Soviet Union. If, then, this model adequately captures the popular mind, evidence of chaotic/impulsive sentiment should be reflected in public opinion on East-West matters. If it is asserted that Americans have been lethargic about foreign threats, attitudes on East-West issues should provide an excellent test of that proposition. If the public has tended to overreact to foreign challenges, this attitude should be apparent here as well. If the public's feelings have been unrelated to international conditions, if they have chaotically bounced from one mood to another, this too should emerge from the data. In any case, it is with regard to U.S.-Soviet relations that claims of both the excesses and the moodiness of mass opinion, claims of the public's alternating complaisance and hostility have most often been made. According to Adam Ulam, "powerful gusts of popular emotion rather than factual data about the international situation determined the main lines of American foreign policy."[29] Kennan concurs, pointing out that "the motivations for American policy toward the Soviet Union from the start have been primarily subjective not objective in origin.

They have presented for the most part not reactions to the nature of an external phenomenon (the Soviet regime) but rather the reflections of emotional and political impulses making themselves felt on the American scene."[30]

Certainly, the history of public feelings toward Russia has been rather tempestuous—periods of surprising affection alternated with periods of sharp animosity; sentiment was very warm during the American Revolution but rancorous at the time of the division of Poland. It was amicable during the American Civil War, chilly toward the end of the nineteenth century. Historical perspective is also needed for the postrevolutionary period of Russian history, for if the public feelings have recently been restrained, such was not their dominant property in earlier decades. Extreme representations of the Soviet Union characterized the years immediately following the Bolshevik seizure of power in 1917—when stories circulated about electrically driven guillotines and Communist-established bureaus of free love.[31] Even at the height of the wartime alliance between the two nations, most Americans had considerable misgivings about Russia, feeling that it was only slightly less unsavory than Nazi Germany.[32] By the mid-1940s the Soviet Union emerged as a menace greater than any the United States had previously encountered, and the nation worked itself into a state of frenzied anxiety over the threat. Though only 38 percent of the public considered the USSR "aggressive" in 1945, 66 percent shared this opinion of their former ally by 1947.[33] While 58 percent felt that Russia was trying to "build herself up to be the ruling power of the world" in 1946, 76 percent thought so in the following year (and only 18 percent believed Russia was "just building up protection against being attacked in another war").[34]

By 1947 more than 62 percent of the public disapproved of U.S. policy toward Moscow, considering it too "soft," a judgment that became even more pronounced in 1948 and persisted into 1949—despite the Truman doctrine and the administration's tough anti-Soviet posture (table 2.2).

Feelings did not temper during the early 1950s. In 1951 66 percent of the respondents felt that in the event of an all-out war with Russia the United States should "drop the atomic bomb on Russia first"; only 19 percent thought that "we should use the atomic bomb only if it is used on us."[35] This readiness to use nuclear weapons in the

TABLE 2.2
Public Perceptions of U.S. Policy Toward the Soviet Union
1947–1949

	Too Soft	Too Tough	About Right	No Opinion
October 1947	62%	6%	24%	8%
March 1948	73%	3%	11%	13%
July 1948	69%	6%	14%	11%
September 1949	53%	10%	26%	11%

SOURCE: The Gallup Poll

event of conflict is especially startling since many Americans believed at the time that war between the superpowers was altogether likely. Despite America's substantial military and economic edge over the Soviet Union, and although no major crises opposed the two countries, in 1954 64 percent of Americans thought that there would be a major war between them sooner or later.[36]

Paroxysms of external anxiety were matched by a feisty intolerance at home. The previous chapter alluded to the campaign against alleged leftist subversives waged by the administration and congressional committees but the average American appeared every bit as pugnacious. From the calmer perspective of the present it is surprising how little concern the public displayed for the First Amendment rights of those whose politics it disagreed with. In 1954, for example, 51 percent of the public felt that "an admitted Communist should be put in jail," while 77 percent agreed that such a person's "American citizenship should be taken away."[37] Although the nature of his methods had become quite apparent, 50 percent of the public in 1954 claimed to have a favorable opinion of Senator Joseph McCarthy, while only 29 percent held an unfavorable opinion.[38]

The evidence of the time gave little support indeed to Reinhold Niebuhr's characterization of democratic politics as "full of illusions about the character of human nature, particularly collective behavior. It imagines that there is no conflict of interest which cannot be adjudicated. It does not understand what it means to meet a resolute foe who is intent either upon your annihilation or enslavement."[39]

Rather, the picture that the U.S. public had painted of itself by the mid-fifties supported the conviction, when the political sentiments of the masses are roused, that emotion eclipses reason, pushing policy toward excesses sobriety would decry; and it supported the belief that "the volatility and potential explosiveness of American public opinion must be constantly kept in mind if panic reactions to threat are to be avoided."[40] By extension, this portrait might have led observers to question, along with most realists, how far political leaders should let themselves be directed by moods that reflect so little balanced judgment.

Still, public awareness has not remained frozen at the level of the early fifties, and the extremes of the past do not necessarily indicate where popular preferences could swing in the future. Political conditions have altered considerably since, and people are generally capable of deepening their judgment and calibrating their understanding on the basis of relevant experience, even if their grasp of specific events remains shallow. A once isolationist nation has been immersed in world affairs for quite a few decades; superpower relations have gone through several cycles of increasing and declining tension, and, despite the continuing low level of factual information held by the public, a pondered awareness of international reality may have seeped into the public consciousness. In any case, the most recent decades have provided few examples of irrational emotionalism in the average American's reactions to the external challenges—especially with regard to the Soviet Union.

Notwithstanding the dramatic deterioration of superpower relations during the early years of the Reagan administration and the precipitous drop in public approval of the Soviet Union since the detente of the 1970s most Americans were not swept up by the wave of governmental belligerence. The majority of those surveyed wanted arms control negotiations, cultural and educational talks, and even joint efforts to solve energy problems.[41] By 1984, while relations were still frigid, 90 percent of those questioned endorsed nuclear arms control talks, and more than 80 percent wanted to expand academic and cultural exchanges with the Soviet Union.[42]

In 1987 a leading student of political opinion reported one half of the public feeling that "we should take a strong position with the Russians now so they won't go any further, but at the same time we should try to reestablish good relations with them." By contrast, only about one quarter adopted the more extreme stance that "we should do nothing that is likely to provoke an American-Russian conflict but instead should negotiate and reason out our differences," or that "it is clear Russia can't be trusted and we will have to rely on increased military strength to counter them."[43] On the whole these appear to be reasonable positions, balancing firmness and a willingness to seek better relations—a far cry from the extremism of the early Cold War years.

Moreover, the U.S. public seems not to display the frequent passivity in the face of foreign challenges that has been lamented as an aspect of its naively apathetic character. If opinion operates in the form of irrational bursts of emotion interspersed with long stretches of complacent indifference, this should have been reflected in the public's attitudes toward the Soviet Union and national defense but little evidence of this can be found. Never until well into the Gorbachev era had even half the public expressed *any* level of approval of the USSR; rather, a cautious wariness emerges from the data. On the other hand, the extreme odium apparent in the fifties has not been in evidence since. On the whole, approval ratings have tracked the state of overall relations between the two nations: improving during the sixties, reaching a high at the time of detente, deteriorating with the collapse of detente in the late seventies and early eighties. When as a result of Gorbachev's policies evidence of dramatic change in Moscow's orientation toward both domestic and foreign policy became amply evident, over 60 percent responded with some level of approval of the Soviet Union (a slightly higher rating than registered, for example, by Israel).[44]

If they have always been in favor of arms control, and, since the Cold War peaked, averse to saber rattling, Americans have traditionally endorsed military preparedness. When asked to list the major factors in America's greatness in 1976, 80 percent of those questioned mentioned military strength.[45] On average, one fifth of the public desired higher military spending; but in 1980, when relations deteriorated and when there was evidence of a substantial Soviet military buildup, 60 percent wanted larger defense budgets. With the dramatic surge in defense outlays during the Reagan administration's first term in office, this figure dropped to its habitual 20 percent.[46] Moreover, while the public in general has not demanded nuclear superiority over the USSR, its willingness to negotiate arms control has been contingent on at least a rough U.S. strategic parity with the Soviet Union.[47] The U.S. public believes in negotiating from a position of strength, but in recent decades it has shown no taste for rabid militarism.

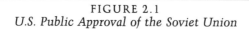

FIGURE 2.1
U.S. Public Approval of the Soviet Union

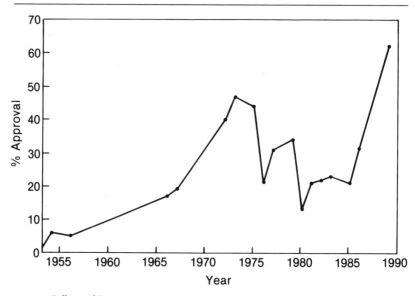

SOURCE: Gallup and Roper

Although most U.S. administrations were probably not considered extreme, two recent presidents were thought to be excessively eager for either cooperation or confrontation with Moscow: Jimmy Carter and, during his first term in office, Ronald Reagan. In 1980 60 percent of the respondents in a Gallup survey felt that President Carter was "not tough enough" toward the Soviet Union.[48] Three years later 56 percent of the participants in a Harris Survey, responding to a question about Reagan's handling of U.S.-Soviet relations, agreed that "he doesn't seem to realize that negotiations to make peace are more important than building up the armed might of the U.S."[49] In line with its distaste for significant departures from middle-of-the-road policies, the public wished to push each of the two presidents away from the extremes to which he sometimes inclined. While the public considered Reagan an obvious hawk, it tended to reward him with increased approval when he acted in a conciliatory manner yet withdraw its endorsement when he displayed his hawkish side. By contrast, public approval of Carter's Soviet policy increased when he seemed to be acting assertively toward the USSR but declined when he appeared overly cooperative.[50]

For example, by May 1984, when relations between the United States and the Soviet Union had degenerated to their lowest level in decades, only 38 percent of the public approved of the president's Soviet policy. But when, several months later, initial efforts at diplomatic fence mending got underway, approval rates began inching upward. In September 1984 Soviet Foreign Minister Andrei Gromyko attended the UN General Assembly meeting in New York and had his first constructive talks with Secretary of State Shultz. Gromyko also paid a call on President Reagan in Washington and the two men decided to reopen arms control negotiations. By October 48 percent of the respondents approved of the way their president was handling the Kremlin. In January 1985 high-level delegations from the two countries met in Geneva, and there appeared the first signs of an authentic thaw in superpower relations. Approval of President Reagan's Soviet policy rose to 60 percent. Ten months later Reagan and Gorbachev had their first summit conference. Although it produced few tangible accomplishments, the summit was conducted in a cordial and cooperative atmosphere and public approval of Reagan's handling of Soviet relations reached 65 percent—the highest level yet.

A very different pattern characterized the public's feelings toward President Carter. During the first months of his presidency, he voiced optimism that detente could be saved, and SALT II and Comprehensive Test Ban negotiations were opened in Geneva. There was even serious talk of bringing the Kremlin into the Middle East peace process. By June 1978 approval of the president's Soviet policy dropped to 28 percent. At approximately this time, his attitude toward Moscow began to change. As his stance became tougher and more critical of Soviet conduct, public approval of Carter's handling of the USSR moved back upward—reaching 43 percent by the end of the year.[51] If Reagan the hawk was most rewarded in the public opinion polls for dovish behavior, while Carter the dove did best when he acted assertively, President Bush, who has consistently pursued a middle-of-the-road policy toward Moscow, has had his handling of the USSR rewarded by consistently high levels of popular approval.

Even if there is no clear dividing line between a stable and unstable opinion, between one that is moderate and one that is extreme, very much of the data supports the conclusion that the public has displayed a reasonable attitude toward America's premier rival. The public is alert to potential threats but displays little of the erratic emotionalism that has been ascribed to it; on the whole, its attitudes have been sensibly grounded in the shifting nature of the Soviet challenge. Rather than driving relations on a perilously volatile course, public opinion is more likely to have had a moderating influence on policy—discouraging both dovish and hawkish extremes. In any case, it is hard to recognize in the American public a creature resembling Kennan's prehistoric monster.

Military Intervention Abroad

We have seen that the U.S. public believes a major component of America's greatness to be its armed might—but just how judiciously is the public inclined to use it? Is it prone to uncritical interventionism at certain times while unwilling to accept the costs and risks of projecting force abroad at other times, as the chaotic/impulsive model would suggest? Neither speculation is in fact accurate; the average American is neither eager to fight in remote regions nor unwilling to consider the use of force when key national interests are demonstrably at stake. Again, not the prehistoric monster who, by virtue of its transports of moods, deserves to be ignored by leaders formulating responses to major international challenges.

Despite the increasing assertiveness of U.S. foreign policy during the Reagan era, which was generally endorsed by a public worried that their country's position in the world had eroded during the 1970s, Americans were wary of a blind reliance on military force. The Reagan administration tried hard to convince the public that Central America was pivotal to U.S. interests—UN Ambassador Jeane Kirkpatrick even proclaimed that it "is the most important place in the world for the United States today,"[52] but the public was not moved to endorse military intervention in that region. Whatever Americans may have thought about the relative merits of the issues or actors in that part of the world—and there is every indication that they knew little about the particulars—they did not consider the stakes worth fighting for. Altogether, 74 percent opposed an invasion of Nicaragua to remove the Sandinista government in 1984, while 72 percent feared that U.S. involvement in Central America could lead to another Vietnam.[53] Despite President Reagan's tireless praise of the Sandinista's domestic opponents the average American was unimpressed and, as late as 1987, nearly three quarters of those asked opposed assistance to the Contras.[54] In fact, most Americans even disapproved of military maneuvers in neighboring Honduras, which were plainly designed to intimidate the Sandinistas.[55]

Although the U.S. public thought ill of Fidel Castro in the early sixties and felt that Cuba was a monumental thorn in America's side, it was not so driven by bellicose sentiment as to support the idea of getting rid of him by force (when asked whether that would be a good idea only 20 percent of those queried agreed).[56] Another example of the public's distaste for military intervention was furnished during the Carter years. When in Teheran U.S. diplomats were held hostage by Iranian militants who occupied the American Embassy and subjected the hostages to a variety of indignities, never did a majority favor the use of armed force to free them.[57] Similarly, despite the U.S. public's deep distaste for Colonel Qaddafi, a majority has never approved the notion of going to war against Libya,[58] and, its antipathy toward Panama's corrupt and repressive General Noriega notwithstanding, in 1989 69 percent opposed the suggestion of ousting him by military force.[59]

Does this mean that the public is weak-willed and apathetic to the point of opposing military intervention, no matter what the circumstances might be? It does not. Where the average American is convinced that crucial interests are at stake, he or she considers the use of force perfectly acceptable. Most Americans have recognized the need for armed intervention to defend West European nations if attacked by the Soviet Union—a majority supported such intervention both in 1981 and 1985.[60] Similarly, a majority has typically upheld the need to send troops to protect U.S. interests in the Persian Gulf; and when a U.S. flotilla was dispatched to the region in 1987 to protect neutral shipping from Iranian attack two-thirds of the public felt that this was a good idea.[61]

Also, and no matter how it might have felt about the idea initially, the public will usually rally "round the flag" once U.S. soldiers are committed abroad. Most Americans were at first unenthusiastic about the idea of sending troops to Vietnam; before the Gulf of Tonkin incident in 1964 only 42 percent supported armed involvement in that part of the world.[62] But as the nation became militarily committed to South Vietnam's defense against both domestic revolution and North Vietnam, the public stood behind its government; in fact, after President Johnson moved to extend U.S. military engagement in Vietnam 72 percent supported the decision.[63] Before President Nixon ordered an invasion of Cambodia in search of Vietcong sanctuaries only 7 percent of Americans surveyed endorsed the idea; but once the invasion began 50 percent expressed their approval.[64] Similarly, although a majority of Americans opposed the notion of invading Panama to deal with Noriega before the fact, President Bush's decision to dispatch U.S. forces for his ouster in 1989 encountered overwhelming popular approval. Public support of military interventions rarely survives a costly and protracted involvement, yet the public is willing, for a while at least, to stand behind its government's decision.

An interesting finding reported by Bruce Jentleson is that while the public was generally disinclined to endorse military engagements abroad during the 1980s, it was much more likely to support the use of armed force in the Third World when U.S. foreign policy interests were demonstrably at stake than when the intervention was designed to affect an internal change in the target country (even when it was a matter of promoting democracy).[65] Thus the public, like the realists who worry about disruption from below, appears guided by a pragmatic notion of the national interest, rather than by an abstract idealism reflected in the zealous propagation of its own political values.

It is hard to find credible grounds for asserting that national moods are either conducive to Rambo-like militarism abroad or for claiming that the public is so hesitant about resorting to force that a major component of U.S. power is neutralized by the flaccid national will. As was the case with popular attitudes regarding East-West relations, the impression is of sentiments that, while mature and restrained, recognize there are some interests that must be defended by military means—of a willingness to give leaders the benefit of the doubt, for a while at least, when they do resort to armed coercion. Moreover, the public's willingness to endorse the use of force does seem based on coherent grounds—the relevance of the countries or regions to U.S. political and security interests.

Our examination of public opinion on East-West matters and on military intervention abroad has not aimed for great analytic profundity. Its task was primarily descriptive—to see what image of the popular mind, as reflected in opinions on two significant foreign policy issues, is revealed by the data. The conclusion is mixed. While opinion polls confirm that the average American is not well informed on external policy, there is no evidence that the public mind is particularly disorganized, unstable, or extreme regarding foreign affairs. On the whole, popular sentiment appears moderate; neither lurching nor volatile, it exhibits what V. O. Key described as "viscosity."[66]

But if the public does not fit the description often provided for it, we may still wonder why the chaotic/impulsive model is not implied by the slim foundation of popular information, and whether factual knowledge is indeed a crucial condition for public participation in foreign policymaking? A good point of departure is to ask if there are not several dimensions to public opinion, each carrying a different implication for the compatibility of democracy and sound foreign policy.

The Complexity of Opinion

Why, despite so general a conviction that the average American's foreign policy beliefs are irrational and volatile, does so much evidence suggest otherwise? Two explanations spring to mind. The first is that, although this description may have been appropriate in the past, the assumptions on which this image rests are *no longer* valid. The second possibility is that these assumptions were misconceived at the *outset.*

If a presumption of excessive public ignorance is at the basis of the chaotic/impulsive model, then it may be that ignorance is a relative matter and, while the average member of the public today is not very knowledgeable on major matters of national concern, that understanding is nevertheless less shallow than several decades ago. Consequently, the judgments that were accurate when observers such as George Kennan and Walter Lippmann formulated their critiques of popular pressure may simply have been transcended. The increasingly rich store of foreign policy experience of a nation that emerged decisively from isolationism half a century ago, as well as a media that has become increasingly sophisticated on international problems, may have deepened public awareness of the issues, imbuing it with greater coherence, moderation, and stability. This may be reflected in what James Rosenau, in a subsequent work, reported to be "a small but steady expansion of the number of citizens who develop and maintain a continuing interest in public affairs."[67] It is also suggested by the observation that the proportion of the US public claiming to be very interested in news about other countries and about U.S. foreign relations has shown a steady rise over recent decades.[68] In other words, if the attentive public is progressively expanding, a citizenry with more firmly anchored and reflective opinions on international affairs could be the result.

But it is also possible that the assumptions behind the model were misguided at the very origin. Apart from its assumption of public ignorance, one of the model's cornerstones is the belief that popular thinking on foreign affairs is not constrained by a coherent *structure* of thought. Under the circumstances, foreign policy beliefs bounce around in an intellectual vacuum, attaining unexpected extremes and displaying abrupt shifts. The social-scientific underpinnings for this thesis were largely provided by Philip Converse's assertion that many views, including those bearing on foreign policy, cannot be predicted on the basis of a knowledge of the person's beliefs on such issues as economic policy or, say, social morality.[69] In other words, foreign policy beliefs are not anchored by a system of *horizontal constraints*, where beliefs within one issue domain are systematically related to opinions within other issue domains such that a coherent philosophy comes to characterize the person's political thinking.

Viewed thus, foreign policy opinions may have some properties suggested by the chaotic/impulsive model, but horizontal constraints are not all that anchor the public's opinions, for they are organized by *vertical* constraints as well. By vertical constraints, we mean those that operate within the same issue domain, and that make specific opinions predictable on the basis of more *general* beliefs within that particular issue area. For example, feelings about a new tax for school construction may be connected to broad feelings about the value of liberal education, or support for a specific U.S. military intervention may be guided by general convictions regarding the legitimacy of armed force as an instrument of foreign policy. Much sophisticated research indicates that vertical constraints are prevalent even where horizontal constraints are not,[70] and what research there is also suggests that vertical constraints do indeed characterize the public's foreign policy views.[71] Accordingly, to the extent that more general beliefs tend to be reasonably stable, beliefs of a specific nature should not be expected to exhibit much volatility.

Because of this, we may doubt that the core assumptions underlying some of the least flattering conceptions of public opinion are valid. And, if our descriptive overview of survey data indicates that these conceptions are wrong, so do a number of methodologically more ambitious endeavors. One article, published in 1970, which examined popular support for external commitments, concluded that the public's response to foreign affairs is surprisingly stable.[72] Moreover, the study that particularly stands out in terms of the range of data examined determined foreign policy opinion to be no more unstable than opinion on domestic matters. According to its authors, "the striking finding is one of general stability," while "the American public has generally responded in a sensible fashion to international and domestic events, as reported and interpreted by the U.S. mass media and by American leaders."[73]

If much of the literature on democracy and foreign policy, especially that grounded in realpolitik, rests on tenuous assumptions about the structure of the popular mind, another flaw is its reliance on an undifferentiated conception of public sentiment. Actually, public opinion has several dimensions and each may have a different bearing on the awareness required by sound foreign policy. Those who comment upon the popular influence on external affairs are rarely explicit about which dimension they have in mind, making a definitive evaluation of their views on democracy and foreign policy elusive. Accordingly, we must describe these dimensions of opinion and ask how they bear on different forms of foreign policy awareness.

There are at least four dimensions to public opinion. One dimension reflects *cognitions* about the world. Another expresses mass *sentiments*, i.e., emotive responses to cognitions. A further dimension involves *aspirations*—desires about the direction policy should take. A final dimension concerns *inferences* (drawn from a combination of cognitions, sentiments, and aspirations) about what the international system is like and how its various components are linked. The point is that different facets of opinion may imply different conclusions about the popular impact on foreign policy. For example, evidence used to demonstrate the public's shallow understanding of foreign policy is generally based on cognitions (as was the case of the data used in this chapter). Conceivably, however, evidence on popular inferences might have led in a different direction. In fact, there is no inevitable relation between the level of public cognition and the quality of its input into foreign policy. As Bruce Russett has noted, a *high* level of information on any policy spectrum is generally correlated with intensity of opinion and intensity of opinion, in turn, is correlated with extreme preferences on the policy issue.[74] In other words, there may be an unfortunate link between cognitions and sentiments (although the former need not account for the latter). Much as those who hold the most extreme views on domestic issues (on capital punishment, for example) are likely to have more relevant facts at their fingertips than those whose positions lie in the middle of the spectrum of beliefs, the same applies to those who hold the most uncompromising foreign policy opinions (e.g., supporters of unilateral disarmament or of outright nuclear superiority).

If good foreign policy need not hinge on extensive factual cognition, it is hard to argue that it does not depend on the correctness of the inferences by which it is guided. But the quality of inferences is not always dependent on the scope and accuracy of cognitions. Some very capable research in political science distinguishes *information* (factual knowledge) from political *sophistication* (based mainly on the quality of inferences), determining that the former need not help predict the latter.[75] It is also useful to recall the observation of Elmo Roper (himself a close student of public opinion) that

> a great many of us make two mistakes in our judgment of the common man. *We overestimate the amount of information he has; we underestimate his intelligence.* I know that during my eight years of asking the common man questions about what he thinks and what he wants I have often been surprised and disappointed to discover that he has less information than we consider vital. But I have more often been surprised and elated to discover that, despite his lack of information, the common man's native intelligence generally brings him to a sound conclusion.[76]

If public opinion is indeed multifaceted and multilayered, how are its various dimensions related to the types of awareness required for the successful conduct of international affairs?

The Matter of Necessary Understanding

Roughly speaking, and related to the four dimensions of opinion, three kinds of awareness shape foreign policy. The first involves *factual* information, including such things as names and places, the substance of issues (e.g., what specific arms control talks are about), and various technical matters (e.g., what is a floating exchange rate or what is the difference between a Minuteman and a Midgetman missile). This knowledge is essential to both routine and momentous decisions, and its acquisition requires much time and incentive.

The second category concerns *normative* understanding, which is generally revealed in public sentiments and aspirations. It involves the ends that, as a nation, we ought to seek and the manner in which trade-offs should be resolved between those that are not wholly compatible. Should we, for example, care about the internal political arrangements of other countries, or merely about their attitudes toward the United States? Should we be more concerned about international peace or prosperity? On some occasions, normative issues require ethical judgments, but not always—frequently they involve a choice between strictly utilitarian ends (e.g., which national goals, if attained, will enhance the utility of most members of the society). In any case, this is the level of awareness that imparts an overall direction to foreign policy.

The third form of awareness concerns the *context* within which the ultimate goals are pursued; it is generally reflected in public inferences and, again, in sentiments. It implies either or both of two types of judgment. The first is of an ontological nature, involving assessments of what the world in which we operate is like. For example, was Soviet Communism inherently aggressive, as foreign policy conservatives have long claimed? Is it accurate to say that developing nations are "ungrateful" for whatever foreign aid we give them? Secondly, and in addition to ontological judgments, contextual understanding bears on the manner in which things are causally connected. For instance, will an increase in America's military power make its adversaries more accommodating or will it simply induce them to increase their own military might? Whether answers given to such questions are right or wrong, they define how the context of foreign policy is perceived, and awareness at the contextual level molds the strategies by which the nation's objectives are pursued.

The tri-level distinction often breaks down in practice. For example, causal understanding frequently requires an adequate store of factual knowledge; normative desires sometimes stem from ontological beliefs and so forth. Still, the distinction is a useful one, and conclusions about the public's foreign policy impact must be based on the respective significance attributed to the various forms of awareness as well as based on the respective advantages assumed for public and government regarding each.

Popular inadequacy is most pronounced at the factual level (as was revealed by the survey data reviewed at the beginning of the chapter) and it is principally this form of ignorance that fuels doubts about the public's ability to guide foreign policymaking. If, for example, many Americans do not know what a given arms control treaty deals with, they cannot provide much direction to U.S. negotiators or sensibly evaluate the treaty's merits. Similarly, if much of the public does not know what the parties to a foreign conflict stand for, it cannot intelligently evaluate the desirability of U.S. support for either side, or sensibly reward its leaders for their policies regarding the conflict.

By contrast, the public's inferiority is slightest at the level of normative issues, for one would be hard-put to argue that political elites appreciate the ultimate goals that the nation should pursue any better than does the average citizen. It is also worth noting that, extant wisdom notwithstanding, the foreign affairs goals of the U.S. public and leadership are rather similar, a finding that seems to be stable over a number of points in time.

The most apparent difference is that the average citizen is more likely to stress the economic ends of external policy, while leaders place greater emphasis on security objectives. Even with respect to the latter, however, the only truly pronounced difference appears when it comes to defending the security of allies (nevertheless, the public has been somewhat more prone to stress the need to contain Communism). On this basis, one could argue that there are ways in which popular preferences match the dictates of hard-nosed realism less closely than do those of political elites. The average citizen also favors strengthening the United Nations more than do leaders, but this hardly amounts to great popular enthusiasm for the world body. On the other hand, the public is very weakly committed to a goal that realists would frown upon most severely: promoting one's own

TABLE 2.3
Foreign Policy Goals for the United States
(Percent of Public and Leaders Saying "Very Important")

	1990 Public	1990 Leaders	1986 Public	1986 Leaders	1982 Public	1982 Leaders	1978 Public	1978 Leaders
Primarily Economic								
Protecting US jobs	65	39	78	43	77	43	78	34
Securing energy supplies	61	60	69	72	70	72	78	88
Protecting interests of US business abroad	63	27	43	32	44	25	45	26
Primarily Realpolitik								
Containing communism	56	10	57	43	59	44	60	45
Defending allies' security	61	56	56	78	50	82	50	77
Matching Soviet military power	56	20	53	59	49	52	**	**
Protecting weaker nations from aggression	57	28	32	29	34	43	34	30
Primarily Idealistic								
Strengthening the UN	44	39	46	22	48	25	47	26
Promoting and defending human rights abroad	58	45	42	44	43	41	39	35
Worldwide arms control	53	80	69	83	64	86	64	81
Improve standard of living in other countries	41	42	37	46	35	55	35	64
Help bring democracy to other nations	28	26	30	29	29	23	26	15

SOURCE: Chicago Council on Foreign Relations

political values in other countries (as evidenced by its feeble interest in promoting democracy, or even human rights, abroad).

Thus, the public's normative goals are actually quite close to the foreign policy preferences of the leadership groups from which policymakers are generally drawn.[77] But even where public and leaders diverge, there are no a priori grounds for viewing the latters' goals as more acceptable than the former's. Where foreign policy preferences are rooted in ethical decisions, it is not clear why the people should be less well-equipped than their government. Even where these preferences have no apparent ethical content, it is hard to explain why the public, speaking for itself, is a less competent judge of what it wants than a government speaking on its behalf.[78]

Are we to conclude that the public ought always to be consulted on the normative ends of foreign affairs but that, because of its dearth of factual knowledge, it should leave the specifics of its pursuit to policy professionals? The appropriate relation between public and government cannot be summarized by so simple a formula, since it misses the uncertainty surrounding the government's advantage over the public at the final one of the three levels of awareness, that involving *contextual* (ontological and causal) knowledge. That political leaders have some sort of an edge seems probable—if only because knowledge at this level depends partly on the very factual information in which the public is undeniably deficient. But the danger, and probably the tendency among political thinkers, is to assume that the gap between people and government is larger than it really is.

Intuitively, it would appear that the experience and professional exposure of policymakers should give them a much better conception of what makes the world operate as it does but this edge is often not apparent. For example, there is no strong evidence that many Western political leaders had a better appreciation of the Nazi threat in the mid-1930s than did the average citizen; and there is no compelling indication that their understanding of the Soviet Union's postwar international concerns was any better than that of the man in the street. Closer to the present, the American people seem to have understood sooner than their government that the intervention in Vietnam was not likely to produce the desired outcome at an acceptable price, and, in recent decades, they have shown more constancy in their assessments of the Soviet challenge than have successive administrations.

Why is it that, despite their experience, governments do not make better contextual judgments? There are, it seems, two reasons. To begin with, a political leader's estimates of the nature of a problem and the best way of dealing with it are not entirely, perhaps not even primarily, determined by his definition of the external situation and the substantive merits of the contemplated policy. Whether in democracies or nondemocracies, state leaders' responses to problems must consider a variety of domestic pressures as well, and such pressures often stem from the interests of relatively narrow segments of society. For example, U.S. policy on agricultural assistance to the Third World must take the interests of American farmers into account; similarly, a U.S. response to political unrest in Poland must consider the feelings of Polish-Americans, as much as the external impact of its policies. In a related vein, the organizational interests of government bureaucracies can rarely be ignored by decision-makers, and these interests may have very little bearing on the actual merits of the resulting response. In other words, government leaders must complement their "analytical" problem solving by "political" problem solving,[79] and this implies that much of whatever analytical superiority they possess is offset by the pressures of the segmental interests to which they must respond.

Even if policymakers were to act primarily on an objective analysis of the external problem, it remains that they frequently do not have enough to go on—either in terms of data or relevant analytical tools. Occasionally, necessary information, particularly concerning the intentions and priorities of other nations, is just not available. Very often, too, governments try to make sense of problems by searching for similarities with comparable situations encountered in the past.[80] But historical analogy, as some historians have noted, is a tenuous and overused analytical tool. In David H. Fischer's words, "Analogical inference itself is powerless . . . to *prove that* because A and B are alike in respect to X, they are therefore alike in respect to Y. Proof requires either inductive evidence that A exists in both cases, or else that a sound deductive argument for the coexistence of X and Y."[81]

In the social sciences, inductive evidence is rarely unambiguously compelling, while we generally lack a credible axiomatic basis on which to construct logically necessary, deductive propositions about the link between cause and effect. Moreover, it has been argued that a reliance on "lessons" of history often leads decision-makers to a premature course of action, before the decision is adequately analyzed.[82] Consequently, and although analogies may sometimes be useful, not too much should be expected of them. Also, in many cases there just isn't anything in the past that is even superficially similar to the problem being faced in the present, which means that the assumed link between policy and outcome must often contain a substantial component of intuition and guesswork.

Because of these limitations on analysis, policymakers of equal apparent expertise often disagree among themselves on the character of the problems they face and on the results that various decisions are likely to produce. As an example, although many members of the Johnson administration were convinced that the bombing of North Vietnam would force Hanoi to negotiate on America's terms, many critics within the foreign policy elite thought that this would as likely stiffen its resistance. For a number of years political leaders have been unable to concur on whether quiet diplomacy or outright sanctions would more effectively induce Pretoria to loosen the grip of apartheid in South Africa. Certainly, there has been little agreement, even among physicists and other professionals, on whether the Star Wars (SDI) program could produce a credible deterrent to nuclear attack.

Rifts among experts on some of the most important foreign policy issues suggest that, even among those who have much factual information, expertise in international affairs is often shallow. Accordingly, when it comes to gauging the probable effects of various policies, the government's edge over its public may be slighter than we usually imagine it to be.

Occasionally, its superior factual knowledge will indeed mean that only the government can make a sensible decision. As an illustration, it is difficult to work out an adequate scheme for verifying compliance with an arms control treaty unless one knows something about the production rates and sites, as well as the physical characteristics, of the weapons covered by the agreement. But often a wise decision depends even more on an accurate grasp of ontological and causal matters—what other nations are like, what consequences various policies lead to, and so forth—than on a knowledge of the factual specifics surrounding the problem. For example, the U.S. public in the early 1980s may not really have understood what either the Contras or the Sandinistas stood for, but it may have had at least as accurate a commonsense appreciation of how much a victory for either side would matter to the United States and of whether the stakes merited the costs and risks of military entanglement. Similarly, the average person will rarely have an informed opinion on the ultimate efficacy of a space-based defensive shield against ballistic missiles; but his or her appreciation of Murphy's Law and estimate of the ultimate consequences of a porous shield may be approximately as good as those offered by the government. It is sometimes asked whether, on difficult issues, policies can be both wise and democratic, but this distinction does not apply to foreign policy as often as might be supposed. Most frequently, public participation is not likely to make policies either more or less wise than would have been the case had government ignored popular sentiment. On matters where decisions require a good grounding in a mass of factual detail, the public will have little to contribute and will, in any case, rarely be eager to make itself heard. But when public input is offered—and we have seen that the U.S. government often responds when it is—it will generally not make policies either better or worse; it will simply make them more *democratic*.

One could argue that public input will often be of no help to governments because the things that the public wants are not mutually consistent. Carl J. Friedrich, for example, deplored the public's tendency to "desire both peace and the things that lead to war."[83] In recent decades, one often heard the complaint that the American people wished to contain Communism but were unwilling to accept the costs and risks of military intervention abroad. Such claims may be accurate but are hardly devastating, since there is nothing unusual about wanting the best of both worlds. Most people desire both low inflation and low unemployment, though the two are often mutually inconsistent; they also want rapid industrial growth as well as a decline in industrial pollution, and so forth. Presumably, political leaders are no different in this respect. The point is that, as long as the public can establish a rank-ordering among its various desiderata, and set the overall terms at which it will accept trade-offs between them, it can impose a logical accountability on its leaders and provide them with adequate guidelines on how to proceed.

Ultimately, then, it may not be generally useful to ask whether the public is temperamentally fit to make sensible foreign policy decisions or even whether it knows enough to do so. The first question appears misguided, the second goes too far. There is little to the argument that the public is, by dint of its nature and the quality of its understanding, ill-equipped to involve itself in foreign policy. In most cases, it is not significantly more deficient than its government, and if it chooses to exert its pressure, policy, in the long-term aggregate, is not likely to either suffer or gain as a result. Prevalent belief notwithstanding, disruption from below is not one of the burdens U.S. foreign policy must bear.

Chapter 3

THE CONDUCT OF CONGRESS

Almost all the defects inherent in democratic institutions are brought to light in the conduct of foreign affairs.   —*Alexis de Tocqueville*

Disruption from below and derailment from above are themes that intersect in the matter of congressional involvement in foreign policymaking. The first theme reflects an extension of misgivings concerning the wisdom of the masses—the assumption being that a representative institution whose members are elected by catering to the whims and uninformed prejudices of the populace will reflect those irrationalities, forcing them into a policy arena where decisions should be guided by the knowledge and ability that only the executive branch can possess. In this regard, much that applies to the impact of public opinion on foreign policy would also pertains to the legislature. The second theme, on which this chapter will focus, centers on the manner in which foreign policy authority is structured at the pinnacle of the governmental system: specifically, on the tug-of-war between the executive and legislative branches of government, whose spheres of power and responsibility are defined by blurred boundaries. Foreign relations, it is often feared, are charted by two navigators whose courses are based on independently selected bearings, impairing America's ability to deal purposefully and cohesively with a refractory world.

Not only does the impact of congressional authority on foreign relations raise more questions than did the issue of public opinion, but the meaning of democracy in foreign relations takes on greater complexity as well. It was not difficult to assume a direct relation between the degree of public participation and the extent to which policymaking is democratic, but the role of Congress in democratic governance is more involved. To the extent that it is a vehicle of popular representation, the connection is straightforward, but, at least in the U.S. conception of desirable government, the congressional role is also one of offsetting the power of the other two branches of government—the presidency in particular. The American, unlike the European, view of democracy does not assume that the legislative body, as an expression of popular sovereignty—should control the other branches of government, but that each should check the others—an objective achieved by assigning them different responsibilities and by devising a system of shared, or concurrent, powers. Nevertheless, the specifics of the system remain ambiguous when it comes to international affairs, and considerable controversy surrounds the proper foreign policy roles of the legislative and of the executive branch, respectively.

Perhaps for the last time, the early postwar decades witnessed a significant consensus of foreign policy views between the legislature and the presidency—a comity rooted in the new internationalism and staunch anticommunism informed by prevailing interpretations of the Soviet threat. One should not, of course, overstate even that climate of political harmony; for example, President Truman faced sharp Republican criticism on his China policy, and domestic politics forced him to compromise on his plans for postwar recovery aid to Western Europe. Nevertheless, the willingness to marshall political forces behind executive leadership was greater at the height of the Cold War than at most times before or since; and the departure from norms of domestic power distribution were readily accepted as the consequence of a higher necessity. As Senator William Fulbright reasoned, "The price of democratic survival in a world of aggressive totalitarianism is to give up some of the democratic luxuries of the past."[1]

With the Vietnam misadventure, however, Congress began to re-think its abandonment of foreign policy authority, and a tide of legislative assertiveness gathered momentum. In 1973 Senator Sam Ervin declared that Congress should recapture its "primary respon-sibility for the determination of substantive foreign policy,"[2] while Senator Fulbright now explained that "only if one subscribes to the cult of the 'strong' Presidency which mesmerized American political science in the 50s and early 60s can one look with complacency on the growth of Presidential dictatorship in foreign affairs. . . . [It] was possible to forget the wisdom of the Founding Fathers who had taught us to mistrust power, to check it and to balance it, and never to yield up the means of thwarting it."[3]

The Case Act of 1972 and the War Powers Act of 1973 were the first significant postwar attempts to curb the president's foreign policy autonomy, and by the mid-seventies continuing concern about ex-ecutive abuses of authority prompted additional congressional stric-tures on presidential independence: controls on arms exports, barriers to U.S. participation in the Angolan conflict, and the legislatively mandated promotion of human rights abroad.

Recent surges of congressional assertiveness are especially signif-icant insofar as they have been associated with unhappiness over the substance of foreign policy—as well as with a desire to recapture the foreign policy authority that, in its view, the Constitution had in-tended for it—rather than with historically routine swings of power between the two branches of government. Comparing, for example, the percentage of times Congress voted in favor of a position also supported by the president on a general cross section of congressional votes with the percentage of time it did so on the specifically external policy issues of foreign aid and defense spending, we find that the two have not moved in particularly close tandem (figure 3.1). In the early sixties, for example, agreement between the two branches of government in the two foreign policy areas declined, while *overall* presidential-legislative concordance improved. Similarly, little rela-tion between general and foreign policy support was apparent in the late seventies, although they moved pretty much in lockstep during the eighties.

Thus, congressional willingness to claim its foreign policy prerog-atives should be recognized as more than a generalized reflection of

The Conduct of Congress

FIGURE 3.1
Presidents' Success on Votes in the House

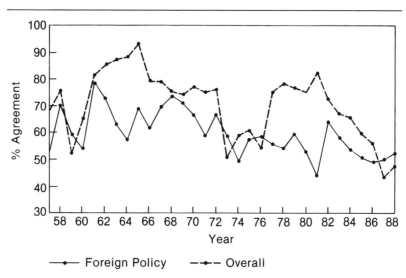

SOURCE: *Congressional Quarterly Almanac*

the state of congressional-executive relations. As such, differences in
their respective frames of foreign policy reference may persistently
intrude on the conduct of U.S. foreign policy—raising pressing questions about the relation between the structure of political power
within the United States and the conduct of the nation's external
affairs.

Predictably, American presidents have resisted assertions of legislative authority. Richard Nixon blamed congressional unwillingness
to support his military policy in Vietnam for the fall of Saigon and,
more generally, for the decline in America's international position.
In his view, "The war and the peace in Indochina that had been won
at such cost over twelve years of sacrifice and fighting were lost within
a matter of months once Congress refused to fulfill our obligations.
And it is Congress that must bear the responsibility for the tragic
results."[4]

Henry Kissinger complained that the War Powers Act weakened
his hand when negotiating with Soviet ambassador Dobrynin over
the war in the Middle East,[5] and he felt that the Jackson-Vanick

Amendment to the 1973 Trade Reform Bill, curtailing the benefits to the Soviet Union of economic commerce with the United States, contributed substantially to detente's demise. President Ford faulted Congress for its attempts to curb the CIA's foreign policy role and for interfering with U.S. policy in Angola.[6] He also charged Congress with undermining the separation of powers by linking foreign aid to the recipient government's human rights performance. "In the final analysis," he observed, "as the framers of our Constitution knew from hard experience, the foreign relations of the United States can be conducted effectively only if there is strong central direction that allows strong central action. That responsibility clearly rests with the President."[7]

Edwin Meese III, at the time President Reagan's chief political adviser, wholeheartedly agreed, announcing in 1985 that "it is the responsibility of the President to conduct foreign policy; limitations on that by Congress are improper as far as I'm concerned."[8]

The consensus of opinion gravitates toward this perspective, estimating that it is the natural mission of the executive branch in general, and of the president in particular, to devise foreign policy strategy and to manage its daily implementation, while Congress should do no more than to trace and monitor executive adherence to its very general outline.[9] In the 1936 case of U.S. v. Curtiss-Wright Export Corporation the Supreme Court concurred almost unanimously, explaining, in the words of Justice Sutherland, that "in this vast external realm, with its important, complicated, delicate and manifold problems, the President alone has the power to speak as a representative of the nation."

Advocates of realpolitik have generally endorsed this view. George Kennan complained that Congress has shown itself able to act on foreign policy "only fitfully" and in "great ponderous lurches" that "greatly limits the flexibility of reaction on the part of the Executive when it does not rule it out entirely."[10] According to prevailing opinion, then, legislators may patrol the outer frontiers of foreign policy but they should not rummage in its daily debris.

A Crucial Trade-off?

No matter how misgivings about congressional participation in foreign affairs may be formulated, their common theme is the presumed lack of congressional expertise and capability on sensitive matters of international politics. The heart of the matter is the apparent trade-off between *competence* and *representation*, the former assumed to characterize the executive branch, the latter viewed as the special province of Congress.[11] If the executive is deprived of sufficient authority, external affairs will be conducted less wisely, but if Congress is not allowed to play a meaningful enough role, U.S. foreign policy will be less democratic. As I. M. Destler observes, "Americans want two things that often prove incompatible in practice: *democratic government* (involving ongoing competition among a range of interests and perspectives) and *effective foreign policy* (which requires settling on specific goals and pursuing them consistently)."[12] The question, for our purposes, is how incompatible these two goals truly are, for views so pregnant with implications should not escape close scrutiny. As a point of departure we must probe the meaning of competence, insofar as it applies to the conduct of international affairs, and ask what inferences are to be drawn for the likely consequences of congressional involvement in foreign relations.

The Matter of Congressional Competence

An Ambivalent Record

The history of the past several decades allows no easy verdict on congressional foreign policy performance, and it is not difficult to muster plausible evidence in support of very different claims on the subject. Examples of ill-considered behavior can be found, but instances of mature discernment and surprising foresight present themselves as well. At times it could have been argued that the national interest would have been better served had Congress uncritically followed the presidential lead. At other times its judgment was probably superior. On some occasions no determinate conclusions on the respective merits of either institution's behavior can be reached, for assessments plainly rest on substantive preferences and ideological inclinations.

It might be observed that two of America's most senseless wars—the War of 1812 and the Spanish-American War of 1898—were largely congressional products. Reacting to public moods and its own thrusts of emotional fervor, Congress incited ventures that historiography has been hard-pressed to justify. At the same time, and with a bovine lack of foresight, it has occasionally demurred when action was required. Despite an authentic opportunity to devise a new international order after World War I, Congress refused to act on establishing a system of collective security as part of the League of Nations. And when the need to put an early stop to Hitler's expansive designs was felt in the 1930s, the mood of Congress (as of the U.S. public) discouraged timely executive action.

More recent examples of apparent legislative bad judgment present themselves. Despite General Douglas MacArthur's complete misestimate of the likely Chinese responses to his escalation of America's involvement in the Korean War, despite behavior that skirted the edges of insubordination to civilian authority, substantial portions of the public and Congress were captivated by his folk hero image, and the administration's sobriety in dismissing MacArthur was not reflected within the legislature. When, following his return home, the general addressed a joint session of Congress with a speech combining patriotism and pathos, senators and representatives openly wept. Representative Dewey Short, echoing the feelings of many colleagues, declared that "we saw a great hunk of God in the flesh, and we heard the voice of God."[13] In retrospect, few would wish that Congress had been granted substantial control over the Korean War.

No event in U.S. history brought the nation, as well as the world, closer to the abyss than the Cuban Missile Crisis. Khrushchev observed that "the smell of burning pervaded the air," while Kennedy estimated that the odds of a disaster claiming some 100 million lives on both sides was "between one out of three and even."[14] Ultimately, the president's combination of firmness and restraint, as well as the Soviet leader's willingness to yield on essentials, enabled both countries to avoid the ultimate calamity—but not everyone favored so reasonable a response.

During a stormy session with congressional leaders in the midst of the crisis, the president's prudence evoked much disapproval. As Robert Kennedy later reported, many in Congress were "sharp in their criticism" of the president. Senator Richard B. Russell, chairman of the Senate Armed Services Committee, declared that "he could not live with himself if he did not say in the strongest possible terms how important it was that we act with greater strength than the

President was contemplating." Even William Fulbright, chairman of the Senate Foreign Relations Committee and a vocal critic of the Bay of Pigs invasion, urged strong military action on the president.[15] In retrospect, it seems fortunate that their advice was not heeded.

Accordingly, instances of misguided comportment by the nation's legislators do exist; but examples of considerable congressional wisdom can also be found. Certainly, the evidence that America's Vietnam involvement had been a mistake impressed itself on Congress before it was recognized by the administration, and many of the nation's doubts regarding the intervention crystallized during hearings conducted by Fulbright's Senate Foreign Relations Committee. In a show of skepticism regarding the wisdom of military solutions to political problems, Congress also restricted the administration's program of military assistance to the Nicaraguan Contras, supporting instead the preference of most Latin American countries for a negotiated settlement to the internal conflict. At the same time it continued to provide humanitarian aid to the Nicaraguan rebels as a way of encouraging the Sandinistas to hold fair elections. On the whole its approach to the problems of Nicaragua may have been more balanced and thoughtful than the more bellicose policies advocated by the Reagan administration. The ultimate unseating of the Sandinistas by electoral methods suggests that the congressional approach was the wiser one. Similarly, it is probable that the 1985 triumph of democracy in the Philippines, and the ouster of Ferdinand Marcos, had much more to do with congressional pressure than with presidential judgment and foresight.[16] The congressional debate in January 1991 on the relative merits of economic sanctions and military coercion for dislodging Iraq from Kuwait was, in terms of sobriety and the range of implications weighed, far more impressive than anything the administration had offered on that issue.

Thus, there have been times when Congress has damaged, or stood to damage, the national interest by forcing itself into the conduct of foreign affairs, but there have also been times when its judgment and preferences corresponded, at least as closely as those of the executive branch, to what hindsight indicates was the desirable course of action. Consequently, the record points in more than one direction and it is only by examining the various components of institutional competence that a meaningful comparison between the two branches of government can be established in this regard.

Two major facets of competence suggest themselves. The first bears on *knowledge* and *discernment*, i.e., on the ability to grasp the nature of external challenges and devise effective policies for dealing with them. The second is associated with *operational aptitude*, i.e., the capability to *act* effectively on the basis of this awareness. In both respects, the executive branch in general, and the presidency in particular, is generally conceded an advantage.

Knowledge and Discernment

Applying the same analytical framework we used to evaluate the public's awareness of foreign policy, congressional knowledge and discernment can be judged from the standpoints of (a) *factual knowledge*, (b) *normative* understanding, and (c) *contextual* (ontological and causal) awareness; we should ask how the legislative and executive branch compare at each level of expertise.

Factual Knowledge At this level, there can be little doubt that the legislature compares unfavorably to the executive; most obviously, because of its inferior resources for acquiring relevant information. The Department of State brings a staff of many thousands of specialists in specific geographic and functional areas to the task of foreign policy analysis, while the Defense Department has over ninety thousand civilian employees devoting their attention to virtually every area of military affairs and national security. The Central Intelligence Agency is the largest and best-equipped intelligence agency in the world, whose resources are complemented by those of the National Security Agency, as well as by those of a variety of more specialized intelligence-gathering organizations. The White House staff, and especially the staff of the National Security Council, provide an additional source of foreign policy information and expertise. In addition, several other executive departments and agencies (e.g., the Department of Commerce, the Department of the Treasury, the Department of Labor) have responsibilities and interests that spill beyond national boundaries.

Focusing, as they primarily do, on issues of direct concern to their constituents, the range of most senators' and representatives' interests is inevitably narrower. A smaller portion of their attention is directed toward international relations, while the staff resources devoted to these matters are comparatively modest. Although many legislators may be competent generalists in international affairs, few—other than those with relevant committee assignments—can claim real expertise in specialized aspects of the field. As late as 1973 Senator Edmund Muskie lamented that the administration was seeking to "spoon feed" Congress "the information [it] decides we ought to have in the way [it] decides we ought to get it, and at the time [it] decides we ought to get it."[17] Had Congress been able to acquire that information independently, the complaint would not have been necessary.

Still, the factual information gap between the branches of government has been shrinking rather than growing. To some extent, this is the result of increased congressional interest in monitoring administration activity and gaining access to the information held by executive agencies. Moreover, recent decades have seen the development of improved in-house capabilities for analyzing international trends and events. The seventies produced a significant expansion of congressional staffs—a development from which the foreign policy, defense, and intelligence committees of both houses have benefited. By the end of the decade personal and committee staffs had more than tripled, in what some authors have described as an "expertise explosion" in Congress.[18] Congressional research units have improved their ability to analyze topics of general foreign policy interest. The General Accounting Office, established in 1921, received expanded responsibilities in the seventies and, exceptionally for an arm of Congress, its International Division has established a number of listening posts abroad. The Congressional Research Service, whose staff more than doubled during that decade, operates an active Foreign Affairs Division. Most recent of the analytical units, the Congressional Budget Office estimates the cost of any bill pending in Congress and of various programs, domestic as well as external, proposed by the administration. The Office of Technology Assessment, created in 1972, is designed to help Congress interpret the policy implications of new technological developments (e.g., Star Wars).

Although the executive branch continues to enjoy some edge in factual knowledge, the implications must not be exaggerated. The acquisition of policy-relevant knowledge usually progresses from the general to the increasingly detailed and specific, and, with certain exceptions, the marginal value of each additional bit of information is more likely to decline than to increase. For instance, it is useful to recognize the character of the factions that confront one another in some geopolitically significant country, but it is less necessary to know the details of their individual organization or of their past histories. It has been more crucial during the Cold War to know the overall military capabilities of the Soviet Union in Central Europe than to grasp the specifics of USSR military training and weapons design. Thus, a diminishing marginal value is usually associated with added increments of foreign policy information, implying that the competence of the two branches of government is not linearly related to the volume of factual knowledge each possesses.

Normative Discernment If the executive branch has some advantage in factual knowledge, the situation is hazier at the other two levels of awareness, for there a greater number of contingent judgments must be made. This is particularly true at the normative level, where the evaluation of each branch of government depends on the foundations on which desirable foreign policy goals are thought to rest. There are at least two ways of viewing these foundations. The first, largely teleological, considers certain aims a priori desirable by virtue of their substance. From this perspective, and using the distinctions introduced in chapter 1, one could either rely on the principles advocated by most realists or invoke goals permeated with a more idealistic content. On the other hand, one could argue that, beyond a few self-evidently crucial needs (e.g., national survival), the desirability of most foreign policy objectives cannot be determined by substantive criteria of an a priori sort, there being no objective standards by which to do so. The solution, then, might be to assume that the appropriate measure of a good foreign policy is given by the process that produced it. Here one would opt for a *procedural* rather than a substantive perspective, estimating that the extent to which an end is worth pursuing is determined by the degree to which the decision to do so rests upon a democratic consensus.

The same distinction could have been invoked with respect to the relative normative awareness of government and popular opinion; but it was less relevant there for two reasons. To begin with, while the U.S. normative and institutional traditions provide guidelines for determining the proper function of Congress, there is less of a basis for deciding what the public's role should be, making a procedural

perspective more difficult to devise. Beyond this, and perhaps surprisingly, there does not seem to be as much divergence on substantive
preferences between the public and the executive as there is between
Congress and the executive (the public's priorities seeming to fall
roughly between those of the two institutions). Accordingly, matters
of normative discernment are not nearly raised so often. The question, then, is what conclusions about the relative foreign policy discernment of the executive and legislative branches of government
flow from either perspective?

A procedural view would probably concede a considerable role to
Congress. Though U.S. political pluralism makes the executive more
than the implementing agent for congressional goals, the country's
constitution (as will presently be argued in more specific cases) pre-
sumes that the legislature is as capable of articulating America's external goals as is the executive branch. Accordingly, we could reason
that a measure of the desirability of a foreign policy is that Congress,
within the limits of its designated role, should concur in considering
it as such.

In this regard, it can also be argued that the normative competence
of the legislative branch may often offset the executive branch's advantage of factual information. This is because many foreign policy
decisions imply a grasp of acceptable trade-offs between wholly or
partially incompatible goals and this, in turn, is largely rooted in the
normative criteria that Congress is called upon to provide. For example, the decision to use or not to use military force in the pursuit
of some national goal would depend on whether the objective at stake
justified the expected cost in human lives. But cost-benefit judgments
of this nature depend not only on the anticipated magnitude of the
human losses (a factual question that, conceivably, the executive
branch can answer more accurately than the legislature), but on the
value of those lives relative to the value of the policy objective—a
purely normative matter that is within the compass of representative
institutions.

However, it is also possible to dismiss the procedural approach to
the validation of foreign policy goals and to assume that certain objectives, being inferentially derived from one or a few central assumptions, are desirable in an absolute sense. Clearly, this is the view
of many variants of realpolitik, wherein appropriate guidelines to

international conduct are derived from assumptions about the nature of political existence. Constitutional rules and domestic political principle cannot alter the need to conform to these guidelines and, if the legislature is unable to do so, its foreign policy role should be restricted accordingly.

In this regard, we must note that the foreign policy objectives of the U.S. Congress are often at variance with what strict realpolitik would endorse—more so, it appears, than is the case of public opinion. For example, congressional insistence during the seventies on making the pursuit of human rights a significant component of foreign policy stood in an uncomfortable relation to the tenets of political realism, and, apart from initial support by President Carter, this emphasis has been opposed by U.S. presidents.

A number of recent congressional initiatives have confirmed a tendency to drift away from hard-nosed realpolitik. The Bush administration had courted China, not only as a quasi ally in the Cold War but as a nation whose restraint in the Persian Gulf was desired (the PRC had been shipping short-range missiles to Iran in the 1980s). Yet after the June 1989 massacre of prodemocracy demonstrators in Beijing the administration, under congressional pressure, was forced to impose a variety of punitive sanctions against China. Its gesture notwithstanding, both the House and the Senate voted an even more comprehensive package of economic sanctions. In the fall of that year, when the administration dispatched a high-level delegation to Beijing to attempt to patch up relations, Congress complained, and as the administration cast its justification in conventional realist terms, Senate Majority Leader George J. Mitchell (D-Maine) responded that "there are times when what America stands for and believes in is more important than economic or geopolitical considerations."[19]

Congressional efforts to use aid as leverage in support of human rights in Sudan and Somalia also clashed with the executive branch's preferences, the administration considering both countries as valuable geopolitical footholds, that should not be alienated by criticism of their domestic practices. Somalia in particular was viewed as an important strategic asset, given U.S. desire for continued access to naval facilities in the port of Berbera, on the Gulf of Aden. But not all congressmen deemed the benefits worth it, seeking instead to make

American economic assistance contingent on greater respect for human rights. As Gary Ackerman (D-NY) asked, "How many human souls is the price of a launching pad?"[20]

During late 1989 and part of 1990 the issue of Lithuania intruded on U.S.-Soviet relations. The Lithuanian declaration of independence incited Moscow's economic sanctions against the republic at a time when the Bush administration, intent on preserving amicably constructive superpower relations, decided to treat the matter of that republic's right to secede as gingerly as possible. Nevertheless, Congress responded by passing resolutions of support for the independence movement and criticizing Soviet attempts at intimidation.

Even in this area executive-legislative differences should not be overstated. Congress couched its resolutions on Lithuania in relatively moderate terms, and it refrained from seeking retaliatory economic measures against the Soviet Union. The sanctions against China contained a clause allowing their suspension by the president, should he deem it in the national interest to do so. Nevertheless, it is apparent that political idealism and realpolitik have sometimes presented themselves as different priorities within the two branches of government.

But one could argue in favor of an executive lead in making normative decisions on completely different grounds—noting that Congress's discernment is twisted by a misguided set of incentives that offset any procedural assumption in its favor. The frequent claim, in this regard, is that congressional priorities collide with the requirements for a wise foreign policy because they are designed to promote the legislators' political fortunes rather than a desirable state of international affairs. Writing in 1932, Walter Lippmann explained that "the chief complaint against Congress, and it is well founded, is that it does not succeed in representing the national interest, that its members are preoccupied with their own special interest in re-election, and that to this end, in an effort to placate, cajole, and even to bribe their constituents, they will as a general rule sacrifice every other consideration."[21]

Others have leveled similar charges but some perspective is needed here. To begin with, even if congressional foreign policy decisions were guided by electoral concerns, this would not distinguish the legislature from the administration. Although the federal bureaucracy is less directly exposed to domestic political pressure than are members of Congress, the difference is one of degree, not kind. Even civil servants are subordinate to a president whose views of the world are filtered through an electoral calculus, as well as to cabinet officers and other political appointees who serve at the chief executive's pleasure and who, consequently, share a similar pattern of political incentives. Members of Congress must tailor their actions to the local—often economic—interests of those who elect them, as demonstrated by congressional support for protection against competing imports or for defense programs that benefit local interests. But presidents (as I will argue more fully in chapter 4) are not very different in this respect. As an illustration, international trade policies at the presidential level are substantially influenced by political pressures—as witnessed, for example, by President Reagan's decision to liberalize grain sales to the Soviet Union in response to farm belt pressures during the 1982 midterm election campaign (while he was pressing U.S. allies to refrain from industrial trade with the USSR). Similarly, presidential policy toward the Middle East has never been entirely divorced from domestic political considerations.

Here, a significant and related paradox generally escapes conventional wisdom. If legislators are driven by concerns that are more parochial than the president's, their foreign policy decisions should actually be *less* politicized as a result, not more so. Their constituencies being particularly interested in issues of *local* import, their stands on foreign affairs are least likely to be guided by electoral calculations—except in the unusual case of an external issue bearing heavily on local ethnic interests.

An early study of the relation between congressional voting records on international matters and constituent opinion on these issues found a very slight correlation between the two—suggesting that, on specific issues of foreign policy, legislators do not primarily seek to please the electorate.[22] By contrast, U.S. presidents are so closely identified in the electorate's eye with international relations that they can rarely escape the electoral consequences of foreign policy.[23] As a result, the superior information base of the president and his administration may not routinely translate into better contextual interpretations for external affairs.

In any case, most instances of congressional insistence on loftier foreign policy values cannot be traced to electoral motivations. Even if we assume that voters were aware of them, it is unlikely that many would have considered their representative's or senators' position on Lithuania, sanctions against China, or assistance to Somalia in deciding how to cast their ballot. Even if they did, the previous chapter found no evidence that political values (such as the promotion of human rights and democracy abroad) rank high on the American public's list of desirable external objectives.

Thus, it is hard to argue that congressional priorities rest on an unworthy set of self-serving political incentives. The ultimate question, then, is whether a procedural or substantive approach is to be taken when deciding on what is normatively valid, and, if the latter, on what sorts of values these objectives should rest—a matter I will discuss more fully in chapter 6.

Contextual Awareness Because contextual awareness generally benefits from factual knowledge, the executive branch starts from a somewhat stronger position than Congress in this regard, but, here again, its advantage may be offset in a number of ways. One important obstacle to contextual awareness, which probably affects the executive branch more powerfully than the legislative branch, stems from the institutional interests and constraints that shape the former's foreign policy interpretations. Officials of executive departments are members of organizations with particular functions, outlooks, and, especially, institutional interests. The leader of an executive department and his deputies may come to their jobs with a variety of perceptions and predilections, but, once they assume their positions, their views come to be dominated by their *roles*.[24] Accordingly, the manner in which they view the outside world is significantly shaped by organizational perspectives and interests.[25]

In addition, institutional self-interest creates political pressures that, while different from those transmitted by the presidency, nevertheless insinuate themselves into policymaking. Struggling to thrust organizational objectives upon national policy, intramural clashes of bureaucratic interests are often created,[26] meaning that views on policy may be the product of competing bureaucratic pressures rather than of objective information. Congressional committees, and their staffs, reflect some of these tendencies as well,[27] but the fluidity of their composition suggests that parochial interests and perspectives cannot as easily take root. Moreover, the institutional link between a congressman and his committees is not likely to be as strong as that binding a bureaucrat to the single organization with which his career is identified. Thus, while the difference is one of degree rather than kind, it cannot be ignored when considering the respective ability of the two branches of government to provide adequate contextual interpretations of international circumstances and foreign policy needs. And the more we probe the differences in knowledge and discernment between the two branches of government, the less convincing is the hypothesis of clear legislative inferiority. If it is to be salvaged, the burden of doing so must rest with criteria of operational aptitude.

Operational Aptitude

Complaining in 1988 about congressional attempts to "weaken my hand," President Reagan echoed a lament he had voiced several years earlier to the effect that "Congress has not yet developed capacities for coherent, responsible action needed to carry out the new foreign policy powers it has taken for itself."[28] He was referring essentially to deficiencies in operational aptitude and, though most would recognize that the Senate does better in this respect than the House, legislative inferiority on this score is rarely questioned.

It is frequently claimed that the size of Congress, and the ponderous pace at which its decisions are reached, disqualify it from participating in the many decisions that require quick and decisive action. The charge has an obvious foundation, but one must ask how *relevant* it really is. No one would seriously suggest that a decision to repel a sudden attack from abroad should require congressional deliberation. Similarly, the business of dealing with terrorist and other egregious provocations often calls for the sort of nimble and covertly planned response that only the executive branch can provide. For example, whether the decision in 1986 to bomb Libya in retaliation for Colonel Qaddafi's encouragement of terrorism was well considered, it was not a decision that could have involved extensive congressional deliberation. Similarly, the 1975 Mayaguez rescue operation, wise or not, was naturally a matter for executive decision. The point, however, is that activities of this character represent a rather small part of the overall foreign policy responsibilities of government, and arguments applicable to infrequently occurring events should not be made to cover a much broader area of international behavior.

An inability to keep secrets is another charge often levied against Congress, with the implication that the executive branch does much better when discretion is called for. But this verdict too stands on a fragile foundation. A number of major leaks of sensitive information have indeed originated from the legislature. In 1976, for example, the controversial Pike Committee's report on the CIA was made available to CBS correspondent Daniel Schorr, ultimately finding its way into the pages of the *Village Voice*. In January 1987 Senator Patrick J. Leahy resigned from the Senate Select Committee on Intelligence, admitting that he had given a reporter unauthorized access to a draft report on the Iran-Contra affair.[29] These and other leaks have attracted considerable media attention, but breaches of secrecy occur at both the legislative and the executive levels, and it is by no means certain that the latter keeps its secrets much better than the former.

Henry Kissinger recalls that, upon assuming office, the Nixon administration had been warned by Presidents Johnson and Eisenhower that "a dangerous practice was growing in the bureaucracy: Some who disagreed with national policy felt free to try to sabotage it by leaking classified information in clear violation of the law."[30] Kissinger was well warned. Leaks of classified or confidential information within the executive branch have often been used to mobilize media and public pressure in support of specific presidential policies, to discredit presidential opponents, and as a weapon of intramural struggle among the various branches of the federal bureaucracy.[31] In any event, Senator Adlai Stevenson III, who served on the Senate Intelligence Committee with responsibility for investigating possible leaks, observed that they were as likely to come from the White House and the executive branch as from Congress.[32]

As one looks below the surface, the trade-off between competence and representation, and the executive's assumed superiority with regard to the former, seem less and less stark. Nonetheless, dominant views on congressional inadequacy shape the role the legislature is encouraged to play, often reducing it to one that is but minimally consistent with requirements of representativity. Though this is apparent in a variety of ways, it is particularly significant in two areas of foreign policy. The first concerns U.S. military involvement in external hostility, the second bears on the international commitments of the United States. Because of their significance, the matter of how decisional authority in these areas is allocated between branches of government probes at the heart of pluralist democracy. Because of their consequence for foreign relations, they bear powerfully on the compatibility of congressional involvement and successful foreign policy. At a minimum, then, it is necessary to ask what allocation of responsibility between the branches of government was intended when the foundations of American democracy were set, and how it has evolved in response to the international role that the nation has since assumed.

The Matter of War Powers

If a procedural approach to determining whether Congress should be called upon to decide the desirability of military engagements is at all useful, it is important to ask whether such a role is or is not provided for in the nation's constitutional tradition. At first glance, the Constitution appears to deal with war powers in a clear and direct, if cursory, fashion. It grants Congress the power to "declare war" (Article I, section 8) as well as, by extension, to "raise and support armies" and to "provide and maintain a Navy." However, recognizing that a body so large and ponderous could not be charged with the operational conduct of hostilities, the Constitution appoints the president "commander in chief" of the armed forces (Article II, Section 2), implying that he has ultimate responsibility for the manner in which the war should be fought. An earlier draft of the Constitution had actually given Congress the power to "make" war, but this was changed to "declare," so that the commander in chief need not wait for congressional authorization to repel a sudden attack on the United States.

Thus, while the president is empowered to begin defensive operations, only Congress is constitutionally authorized to initiate *offensive* military actions. The boundary between the two is sometimes blurred, but the general principle is clear, and it is noteworthy how rarely it has been reflected in historical practice. From Thomas Jefferson's decision in 1801 to send a warship and marine contingent to deal with the Barbary pirates, to George Bush's dispatching of a major U.S. military force in 1990 to the Persian Gulf, the United States has been involved in approximately 130 military interventions abroad. Of those, only five were pursuant to a congressional declaration of war and a only one, the War of 1812, involved a real debate on the merits of the action rather than simple ratification of the president's decision.[33]

Although it is not surprising that American presidents should wish to arrogate most war-making power to themselves, it is less apparent why Congress has not defended its own constitutional prerogatives more zealously. The reason cannot be found in its views of what democracy or the Constitution call for, but in its estimate of the likely *political* rewards and punishments of its actions. A consideration of the matrix of choices typically facing Congress reveals the dilemma.

In the event of a proposed or initiated military intervention, Congress has traditionally encountered two broad alternatives. On the one hand, it could seek to limit the president's freedom to pursue his military objectives by asserting its own authority over such decisions. In turn, this would be associated either with the attainment or the failure to attain his policy goal. Should the military effort be crowned with success, the president would stand to reap most of the political rewards, while Congress could be taken to task for obstructing his efforts. In the event of failure, the president might manage to lay the entire blame on Congress, charging that it had not done enough to protect the lives of troops already committed and that it had shown a lack of determination in dealing with foreign enemies. The fact that a constitutional principle had been upheld would not relieve Congress of the onus of having impeded the attainment of a tangible foreign policy objective. In either case, the assertive legislature stands to come in for blame and criticism.

On the other hand, were Congress to choose the route of submission to executive authority, the immediate political consequences could be appealingly benign. Were the policy not successful, Congress would not expect much blame, having done nothing to restrict the president's freedom of action. By the same token, Congress might not share much of the praise if, given its acquiescence, the objective was achieved. Accordingly, it has been forced to choose between absorbing some criticism for asserting its rights (whether or not the policy objective is attained) or submitting to the presidential will and receiving neither praise nor blame for the outcome. So long as it does not strongly disagree with the substance of the policy, the politically rational decision is to yield on the more general constitutional principle—especially given the presumption in favor of far greater executive competence in this area.

For the most part, of course, Congress has not objected to the actual substance of U.S. military initiatives; especially when they involved, as was usually the case, the promise of significant geopolitical and other benefits, and when, owing to a preponderance of U.S. armed might, they seemed attainable at moderate cost. If congressmen were generally as eager as their presidents to pursue Manifest Destiny and empire during earlier stages of American history, the initial consensus on Cold War issues ensured even greater harmony during the first few decades of post–World War II history.

The Vietnam War undermined the previously unfaltering conviction that the ends of U.S. foreign policy were as virtuous as the nation itself, at the same time that it dispelled the belief that military intervention was a relatively costless enterprise. This, coupled with the realization that a combination of presidential deception and congressional permissiveness had been responsible for one of the most egregious misadventures in U.S. history, led Congress to take the first steps toward recapturing its constitutional powers.

Its major initiative was the War Powers Act of 1973, passed over President Nixon's veto, which required the president to consult with Congress when hostilities threatened to erupt and, if U.S. troops were sent into combat, to report to Congress within forty-eight hours on the likely scope and duration of the hostilities. Unless Congress authorized an extension, these forces were to be withdrawn within sixty days (ninety days under exceptional circumstances).[34] Although the War Powers Act, for the first time, explicitly authorized the president to engage in hostilities without prior authorization, it also established a procedure whereby Congress would maintain considerable control over the ultimate extent of the military engagement. Predictably enough, subsequent presidents have denounced the act as unconstitutional and contrary to the framers' design, and, by invoking two specific arguments, they have sought to create a broader foundation for their power to engage in hostilities without congressional acquiescence.

The first argument is based on the assertion that the Constitution's commander-in-chief clause provides another, independent, source of war-making authority, and, since Richard Nixon's invasion of Cambodia in 1970, it has been claimed to confer the right to *initiate* military action against another country. A former legal adviser to the State Department explained that this designation carries the power "to deploy American forces abroad and commit them to military operations when the President deems such action necessary to maintain the security and defense of the United States."[35]

However vigorously one may argue that the commander-in-chief clause empowers the president to initiate military activity abroad, the justification cannot be found in the U.S. Constitution. The paucity of discussion at the Constitutional Convention about this presidential designation implied, as Frank and Weisband have pointed out, that "the power was not intended to be of much consequence."[36] What evidence there is regarding the purpose of the framers suggests that the authority flowing from this designation was to apply to the operational conduct, not the initiation, of hostilities. Alexander Hamilton, writing in the *Federalist* no. 69, observed that the authority "would amount to nothing more than the supreme command and direction of the military and naval forces as first General and admiral of the Confederacy."[37] The Supreme Court has since agreed. Commenting on the power conferred upon the president by the declaration of war in *Fleming v. Page*, it explained that the commander-in-chief clause implied that "his duty and his power are purely military."[38] Similarly, in 1952 when President Truman ordered governmental seizure of the steel industry to ensure the flow of steel to war industry, justifying his authority to do so by the commander-in-chief clause, Justice Jackson commented that this designation amounted to no more than a "loose appellation" intended to give the president "the command functions usual to the topmost officer of the Army or Navy."[39]

In Arthur Schlesinger, Jr.'s interpretation of the original intent behind the clause, "The Commander in Chief would have no more power than the first General of the Army or the first Admiral of the Navy would have as professional military men."[40] Similarly, Louis Henkin has observed that "the President's designation as commander in chief . . . appears to have implied no substantive authority to use the armed forces, whether for war (unless the United States was suddenly attacked) or for peacetime purposes, except as Congress directed."[41]

Nevertheless, this designation is routinely invoked as the source of war-initiating authority and, in some unexpected cases, for more general foreign policy authority. For example, at a time when Congress criticized President Bush's overtures to China despite its human rights violations, Secretary of State James Baker argued that leadership on this issue "should come from the president *as commander in chief* and as one who is thoroughly versed in the affairs of China" (emphasis added).[42]

There is, moreover, a second aspect to the president's constitutional role from which a power to initiate military activity has been inferred. In addition to being commander in chief of the armed forces, the president is the nation's chief executive, and it is accepted that foreign affairs is largely an executive function and that military coercion is an instrument of foreign policy. Moreover, since some levels of military engagement fall *short* of actual war, a semantic twilight zone in constitutional interpretations of war powers has appeared, a zone in which some uses of armed force may enjoy a special status in the scheme of democratic policymaking.[43]

The growing range of international events that the United States has found itself wishing to influence implies the need for a broad spectrum of coercive as well as noncoercive foreign policy tools. The Constitution's framers, one might argue, could hardly have anticipated the extent of this need and, had they been able to do so, would not have rigidly limited executive ability to act on it. Moreover, while any reasonable conception of democracy requires popular control, through its core representative institutions, of a decision as pregnant in implications as an involvement in actual war, it is not apparent that the same applies to more limited military engagements.[44] Accordingly, one might further argue, a unilateral presidential decision to use armed force would not run afoul of democratic and constitutional principle as long as the operation fell short of a major and protracted engagement requiring substantial mobilization of national resources.

According to W. Taylor Reveley, "We should recognize that . . . some uses of force do not amount to 'war' in the constitutional sense, and leave them wholly within presidential control; these uses involve applications of force that have little human or economic cost for this country and do not impair the sovereignty of another country under current concepts of international law."[45] While one might wonder what use of force abroad would not, in some way, impair another country's sovereignty; there are indeed coercive activities that could be described as "police actions," which should, perhaps, come within the ambit of presidential foreign policy powers. John Norton Moore, a legal scholar and former State Department legal adviser, has maintained that "Congress has exclusive authority to declare war, but it erred in the War Powers Resolution in implicitly denying presidential authority to use armed forces abroad in settings short of war."[46]

The argument may or may not be constitutionally compelling.[47] Louis Henkin, for example, feels that Congress's "power to control war includes the power to control things closely connected to war."[48] More significant, the distinction between police actions and war is rarely tenable on practical grounds. Since the progression from show of force, to police action, to all-out war is continuous, with no obvious points of transition between them, definitional ambiguities lead to increasingly and self-servingly restrictive definitions of actual war by U.S. presidents. Once the principle of military intervention short of war is accepted, it becomes difficult to claim, in any but the most blatantly obvious instances, that the definition of war has, at some point, been met. For example, President Reagan refused to admit that the threshold of war had been reached for American forces in Lebanon in 1982 and 1983—although the U.S. Navy was shelling coastal positions and although 241 American soldiers died in a terrorist attack on Marine barracks in Beirut. In the opinion of many he was wrong to deny reality, yet, as long as the burden of proof lies with Congress, the difficulty of limiting presidential autonomy is apparent.

The principal danger is not that chief executives will consciously leap into wars by denying the meaning of their decisions; the greater peril is that an engagement lying obviously short of war at the outset will escalate, with incremental yet uncontrollable momentum, to a military entanglement with substantial human and economic costs. History provides few examples of wars whose ultimate extent was accurately foreseen by its initiators. Certainly the war in Korea, as well as the Vietnam War, were initially conceived as limited police actions by the presidents with whom they were associated.[49] Accordingly, unforeseen escalations of limited military engagements remain a permanent likelihood. While there may be a point below which the possibility of escalation to war is so remote as to make this a frivolous concern,[50] the burden of proof should, it seems, rest with the president.

One might argue that the distinction between war and military action short of war should stand nevertheless, since Congress retains its ability to curtail an unacceptably escalating involvement by withholding funds. But this argument misses a fundamental point. Congress, like the incumbent administration, must then make its decision under the pressure of sunken costs and committed credibility. In other words, Congress is forced to decide under constraints to which it previously might not have been subjected and would, with timely action, have avoided facing. Additionally, it is in the politically painful position—often deftly exploited by presidents—of seeming to deny the chief executive the means of victory and of protecting those troops that have already been deployed. The Constitution's intent, and presumably the essence of democracy, is to enable representative institutions to control decisions within their purview while they are relatively free to judge the merits of alternative courses of action. A democracy of faits accomplis cannot be the objective, although it might still be argued that in some cases the national interest supersedes political principle.

In this regard, most arguments for an expansive conception of presidential war powers assume that the executive branch has a vast superiority in those abilities requiring the judicious application of force—i.e., understanding of the issues, unity of purpose, ability to maintain secrecy, and so forth. Yet as we have seen, it is easy to overstate this edge, and while there are certain things that the president or federal bureaucracies can do better than Congress, the executive's advantage often falls short of what is claimed on its behalf.

It is important that those who devised the Constitution seem not to have had much doubt about their own purpose. In 1789 Thomas Jefferson wrote to Madison, "We have already given, in example, one effectual check to the dog of war, by transferring the power of declaring war from the Executive to the legislative body, from those who are to spend to those who are to pay."[51] Madison also had strong feelings on the subject. Writing as Helvetius in the *Gazette of the United States* in 1792, he pointed out that "those who conduct a war [the executive as the commander in chief] cannot, in the nature of things, be proper or safe judges whether a war ought to be commenced, continued or concluded. . . . In no part of the Constitution is more wisdom to be found than in the clause that confides the question of war and peace to the legislature, and not the executive department."[52]

Of course, the Constitution is a living document; America's international role, and the challenges it implies, could not have been anticipated by the framers, who might otherwise have accorded the president more latitude in the use of force than they were willing to concede at the time. Moreover, it can be argued that constitutional provisions should be adapted to current circumstances, not to those of the late eighteenth century.[53] The argument seems powerful but it rests on a questionable assumption—that evolving international conditions affect the responsibilities of one, but not of the other, branch of government. The issue is the following: even if growing international challenges imply that the absolute powers of the executive branch should increase, it is not evident that they should expand *relative* to those of the legislative branch—unless it could be argued that the legislative branch lacks both the knowledge and discernment, as well as the operational aptitude, to make sensible decisions on matters of military force. If, as seems likely, this is not an accurate description of legislative abilities, congressional authority to curb the misuses of force should expand in approximate proportion to the frequency with which force may have to be used. Certain scenarios of nuclear war initiation preclude a congressional role, making this an instance where military technology has successfully reduced the scope of democracy; beyond this, arguments for executive autonomy fail to carry much conviction.[54]

International Agreements and Commitments

If Congress should share decisional authority over important national policies other than those that by their very nature must remain the executive's monopoly, then many of America's international commitments logically ought to be subject to this discipline. Such, apparently, was the reasoning of the founding fathers. Although they did not feel that the House of Representatives should be involved in the treaty-making process, the requirement that a two-thirds majority of senators present must agree with the treaty indicates their unwillingness to allow the president to contract international obligations on his own.[55]

This reticence is understandable on two grounds. First, it was apparent that international commitments could have momentous implications, and thus should be covered by the principle of checks and balances; second, it was understood that a treaty is not only an international contract but also a source of legislation. Article VI, section

2 provides that, like the Constitution itself and the laws made pursuant to it, treaties "shall be the supreme law of the land," and lawmaking is a natural congressional prerogative.

Nevertheless, ambiguities remain embedded in the Constitution. The specific content of *advice and consent* is not defined, and the meaning to be given the term has been pretty much left up to the chief executive. Recently, however, chastened by the experience of the Treaty of Versailles (which had been negotiated with very little Senate input), presidents have made a practice of including key senators in the negotiations preceding major treaties—either as members of delegations (as in the SALT process) or as informal consultants. The more significant ambiguity involves the meaning of the word *treaty*, since historical practice has sanctioned various levels of agreements, some of which have fallen short of a treaty in the sense of the U.S. Constitution.

Commitments other than treaties are a matter of practical necessity, for the international business the United States must conduct is too voluminous to be exclusively shaped around agreements that require a protracted process of domestic ratification. Even if it had no other obligations, the time and resources of the U.S. Senate would not be equal to the task of examining and debating the separate merits of every international compact needed for the management of foreign affairs. Hence the justification for executive agreements undertaken at the instance of the executive branch alone.[56]

A large number of executive agreements cover routine and non-controversial matters with which the Senate has neither the inclination nor the ability to involve itself—consular accords, for example, or customs pacts. A number of covenants, on the other hand, deal with issues of greater consequence. In 1817 President Monroe concluded, by executive agreement, an accord with Great Britain on limiting naval deployments on the Great Lakes. President McKinley established the terms for ending America's war with Spain by a similar instrument. Theodore Roosevelt contracted with Santo Domingo to place its customs houses under American control by executive agreement, and secretly acquiesced in Japan's decision to establish a military protectorate over Korea in the same way. In 1940 Franklin D. Roosevelt agreed to lease destroyers to Great Britain (which was under increasing threat from Nazi Germany) in exchange for several British naval bases in the Caribbean. Although this was a significant step toward American involvement in World War II, the agreement was made solely by means of a presidential signature. The 1974 Vladivostok Accord with the Soviet Union on offensive strategic weapons also took the form of an executive agreement.

Not only has the number of executive agreements entered into by the United States expanded considerably but the ratio of agreements to treaties has surged as well. According to one study, the first fifty years following independence witnessed 87 international compacts, of which 60 were treaties. During the next half-century, there were 215 treaties but 238 executive agreements.[57] The trend has persisted into recent decades. At the conclusion of World War II, in 1945, 54 executive agreements and 6 treaties were signed. By 1986 the numbers were 400 and 17, respectively.[58]

Although the Constitution (Article I, section 10) does refer to "agreements and compacts," the specific standards for distinguishing between treaties and executive agreements are blurred. From the perspective of international law, they are interchangeable, the provisions

FIGURE 3.2
Executive Agreements vs. Treaties

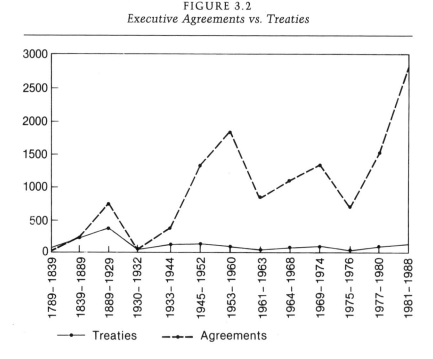

—•— Treaties   —•— Agreements

of both being equally binding on the signatories. In addition, the Supreme Court has held, in *United States v. Belmont* and *United States v. Pink* that, like formal treaties, executive agreements are the law of the land.[59] Initially, it seemed that the distinction might lie in the nature of the matters covered by the two forms of agreement. Emmerich de Vattel, the eminent eighteenth-century jurist, specified that the difference resided in how recurring the obligation implied by the accord was. In the case of treaties, "the acts called for must continue for as long as the treaty exists," while agreements applied to cases in which the obligations were "fulfilled by a single act."[60] Yet as some of our examples have shown, this is not the basis on which the distinction has rested in American history. Louis Fisher is content to observe that the "precise boundary between treaties and executive agreements has never been defined to anyone's satisfaction."[61] Others, more cynically perhaps, have felt that "the executive agreement is an undeclared treaty which, like an undeclared war, seeks to avoid paying its constitutional dues by changing its name."[62]

Because so many of America's external agreements escape the "advice and consent" of the Senate, which frequently has not even been informed of their existence, their scope bears heavily on the compatibility of U.S. foreign policy with the principles of domestic political organization. In this regard, it is important that two categories of executive agreements pose no meaningful threat to these principles. The first are agreements that are made pursuant to an act of Congress or to an established treaty.[63] Examples would be an international agreement sought to comply with domestic law (e.g., regarding drug control) or implementing the provision of an international treaty ratified by the Senate (e.g., a military basing agreement pursuant to the NATO treaty). The second class of legitimate executive agreements are those made in accordance with foreign policy powers explicitly granted the president by the Constitution (e.g., the power to recognize foreign governments or to settle claims for or against the United States).

Beyond this, one might feel that two conditions place an issue squarely within presidential ambit. The first is that it should involve a matter of routine governmental administration of insufficient moment to justify intervention by the legislature. The second is that it should require qualities of knowledge or operational aptitude in which the Senate is plainly deficient. But stating these conditions resolves very little since, as we have seen, the president and Congress often have divergent ideas on what should routinely be encompassed by executive prerogative and on where their respective strengths and weaknesses reside. In any event, these criteria are not very well reflected in the historical record.

In one of the most systematic studies of executive agreements available, Loch Johnson compared their prevalence across various areas of U.S. foreign affairs.[64] For this purpose, he devised an Executive Agreement Index (EAI) representing the ratio of executive agreements to total international accords (executive agreements plus treaties). This was done for the period 1946–1972. Table 3.1 (based on his findings) displays some unexpected and revealing results.

Most striking for our purposes is the *inverse* relation between the apparent significance of the type of agreement and the likelihood that Senate advice and consent would have been sought. The highest EAI was primarily associated with military agreements, the next highest with diplomatic agreements. By contrast, the less politically pregnant areas of international cooperation had relatively modest EAIs. Intuitively, the *opposite* might have been expected. Functional and administrative agreements seem to require the sort of specialized factual knowledge that the executive rather than the legislative branch is most likely to possess. Moreover, their generally routine character leads to the suspicion that, by submitting them most frequently for Senate ratification, the legislature is inappropriately drawn into the day-to-day conduct of foreign affairs—the level of participation for which it is least suited. At the same time, both military and diplomatic

TABLE 3.1
Executive Agreements Index: 1946–1972*

President	Military	Diplomatic	Economic	Transp.-Commun.	Cultural-Technical
Truman	.67	.72	.42	.25	.38
Eisenhower	.84	.71	.12	.39	.55
Kennedy	.83	.41	.27	.86	.67
Johnson	.88	.71	.52	.26	.46
Nixon	.74	.58	.77	.53	.66
Average	.79	.63	.42	.46	.54

*Adapted from Loch K. Johnson, *The Making of International Agreement: Congress Confronts the Executive* (New York, 1984), p. 25

accords involve foreign policy objectives and matters of basic strategy—the very areas where legislative competence may be most pronounced. Perhaps one could claim that the need for secrecy disqualifies the Senate from considering some military agreements, but this would generally not be true of diplomatic agreements.

In 1975 Senator Lloyd Bentsen complained that, in recent years, the executive branch had acted by executive agreement on such major security issues as U.S. military facilities on the India Ocean island of Diego Garcia, naval facilities in Bahrain, and base rights in the Azores. At the same time, the executive branch had dutifully submitted to the Senate treaties on such "relatively less important issues" as the dumping of wastes at sea and protecting producers of phonograms.[65] In 1972 another senator complained, "We are not put in the Senate to deal only with treaties on copyrights, extradition, stamp collections and minor questions of protocol. If that is the meaning of the Constitution, then I think the Founding Fathers wasted their time."[66]

But this is probably not what the founding fathers intended, nor does it follow from what we know about the respective foreign policy competence of the two branches of government. It can be reasonably argued that certain very specialized issues of international cooperation require a factual awareness that escapes many legislators, but these are not the sorts of issue where they have sought to make their voices heard. Nor does table 3.1 suggest that this is the major type of issue covered by executive agreement. Many congressmen came to suspect that executive agreements had become a routine vehicle for the exercise of ungranted presidential power. As early as 1953, Senator John Bricker, a conservative and isolationist, fearing that U.S. membership in the United Nations could lead to agreements with leftist regimes, introduced a resolution to amend the Constitution, empowering Congress to regulate all treaties and other international agreements. The resolution failed to acquire the needed two-thirds majority in the Senate by a single vote. Nevertheless, the Vietnam experience and decreased tolerance for executive autonomy led to a resurgence of congressional sentiment against executive agreements.

In 1969 a subcommittee of the Senate Foreign Relations Committee headed by Stuart Symington launched an investigation of existing U.S. commitments, discovering that their number and import was far greater than previously suspected, sometimes involving major security guarantees of which Congress was unaware. That year, Congress passed the National Commitments Resolution, stating that external commitments should result "only from affirmative action taken by the executive and legislative branches of the United States Government." In 1972 this was followed by the Case Act (named for Senator Clifford Case, R-NJ) requiring that the Congress be informed of all agreements within sixty days of their signing. If the president determined that national security so required, disclosure could be limited to members of the Senate Foreign Relations Committee and the House Foreign Affairs Committee.

Even this did not resolve the issue, for, as no formal definition of executive agreement had been provided, a number of executive commitments were made but not given this designation. The most notorious example was President Nixon's promise to South Vietnam's President Thieu that any violation of the 1973 cease-fire agreement would be met by "full force." Congress was not informed of this open-ended assurance of military support, the president explaining that it amounted to a "statement of presidential intent" rather than an executive agreement. In 1975 Les Aspin complained that since the passage of the Case Act between 400 and 600 accords had been concluded that were not designated as executive agreements and hence not transmitted to Congress.[67] As one commentator concluded, "An executive agreement is what the President says it is."[68]

Amendments to the Case Act and executive-legislative negotiations have since narrowed the administration's discretion to decide what should be designated as executive agreement.[69] Still, an important concern persists: while the transmittal requirement discourages the covert conduct of foreign policy by executive fiat, it does not address the equally significant matter of prior congressional consent to America's international commitments.

On the whole, questions about appropriate authority over America's international commitments do not lead to the conclusion that increased congressional oversight in this area would impede the quality of foreign policy. If the range of the nation's international commitments makes it difficult as a practical matter to fully involve the legislature in their ratification, then this says more about the consequences of so vast an array of external interests on the institutional structure associated with the American conception of pluralist democracy.

The Issue in Perspective

Two questions have run through this chapter. The first regards the consequences of congressional involvement for the quality of U.S. foreign policy; the second concerns the impact of America's foreign policy on the role that the original conception of U.S. democracy assigns to Congress. Although we have not found much to fear on the first score, there is some cause for concern on the second.

Neither the record of recent history nor an examination of the various facets of competence in foreign policy suggest that Congress is as incapable of addressing international problems as is often assumed. And what independence Congress does display on foreign affairs should be seen as part of the normal play of democratic pluralism. It is true that the frequently tempestuous relationship between president and Congress makes it harder to present both friends and enemies with a unified national stance. If this means that foreign policy goals will sometimes not be attained, the logical implication is not that Congress is obstreperous and misguided—the implication is simply that a democratic consensus failed to regard the policy as sufficiently desirable. If, nevertheless, the congressional role is considered unwelcome, this sentiment must rest on the observer's notion of a good foreign policy and his or her conviction that this conception is proper to the executive alone—a conviction strong enough to argue in favor of compromising democratic standards.

Ultimately, then, one's view of congressional foreign policy involvement will depend on normative as well as empirical judgments. If one favors the firmer executive adherence to realpolitik over congressional combinations of geopolitical calculation with attempts to promote Western political values in other nations, then the question becomes one of relative priorities. If the deficient foreign policy competence that realists often attribute to legislatures is not truly apparent in the U.S. case, the remaining question is simply which priorities, executive or legislative, better encompass the national interest. This, in turn, directs us to the question of whether there is a compelling and absolute measure of the true national interest, a question whose consideration will be deferred to chapter 6.

Chapter 4

ELECTORAL POLITICS
AND THE WATER'S EDGE

Democracies decay, if they do, not because of the cupidity of the masses, but because of the stupidity and self-seeking of leadership echelons.   —V. O. Key

If the theme of disruption from below rests on foundations more fragile than those claimed on its behalf, other points of friction between democracy and foreign policy cannot be dismissed. We recognized that struggles between the presidency and the legislature sometimes impair the cohesiveness (though not necessarily the substance) of foreign policy. In a manifestation of derailment from above that is even harder to ignore, external policy may suffer the consequences of the pattern of incentives associated with democratic political competition—a problem with few apparent remedies. The issue is the following: although democratic political competition promotes a relatively effective aggregation of disparate interests and beliefs, its demands sometimes collide with those of statesmanship and, when this happens, the needs of the nation may be sacrificed to partisan politics and short-term electoral advantage. Morgenthau assumed that, unfettered by public pressure, political leaders would take a long-term view of the national interest and conduct the nation's foreign affairs accordingly, in a spirit of sober realpolitik. That the leaders, in the normal play of politics, might be part of the problem rather than the solution has been less often recognized.

The quandary may be especially pronounced in the United States, given the extent to which foreign policy intrudes upon domestic politics. External affairs may be politicized in Greece, England, France, or Germany as well, but this is usually because a particular issue (e.g., U.S. military presence, a dispute with a neighbor) temporarily claims a share of the political spotlight. In the case of a nation that, like the United States, identifies its national interest with a broad range of international outcomes, the hold of partisan politics over foreign affairs is more permanent and powerful. Many Americans believe that even though policies directed internally may be hostage to electoral pressures, a disinterested pursuit of the national interest should guide the government's dealings with the outside world. But this may be too optimistic a view of what domestic political reality normally permits, and two empirical matters should be addressed: (1) the extent to which U.S. foreign policy has indeed become politicized, and (2) the consequences of politicization for the way policy is conducted.

Electoral Competition and Foreign Policy

U.S. foreign policy's entanglement in domestic political struggles occurs mainly in the context of races for the presidency (the political fortunes of representatives and senators being more closely linked to the local interests of their constituents than to international affairs). Although we must ask to what extent presidential candidates tailor their foreign policies to expected political dividends, a logically antecedent issue must first be raised. Since votes are the major prize sought in democratic political contests, some link between votes and foreign policy must exist if external affairs are to be put to electoral use. Do significant electoral consequences indeed flow from the foreign policy behavior of presidential candidates?

As observed in chapter 1, the average American's interest in national affairs is usually sporadic and shallow. When aroused, it is more likely to involve domestic issues—especially those of an economic nature—than international relations. So if the electorate is not likely to care much about its leaders' foreign policy behavior, one may see no reason why presidential decisions in this area should be swayed by electoral calculations. Nevertheless, the evidence indicates that leaders' performance in external affairs can have significant electoral implications, tempting them to tailor foreign policy positions to short-term political ends.

Although there is some disagreement as to what impels a person to vote for one candidate or another, broad categories of influences have been identified.[1] Apart from party identification, the importance of which appears to have declined over the past few decades,[2] voting decisions are based predominantly on a combination of voter feelings about a candidate's stand on issues and more subjective criteria associated with the candidate's personality and character. Political scientists are divided about the relative weight that should be assigned to these two classes of considerations—some stressing the role of issues, others placing a greater emphasis on candidate image[3]—but most recognize that the average voter cares about both. Moreover, there are circumstances in which one or the other is likely to be more important. For example, in a campaign with few substantive issues or in which the candidates adopt similar policy positions, candidate image is especially likely to influence voters' choices. And, it has been demonstrated that image is more likely to matter where challengers are concerned, while issues tend to mold evaluations of incumbents.[4]

Even if it is not likely that foreign policy plays a dominant role in the average citizen's voting decisions, it is probably not irrelevant to the outcome of many presidential campaigns characterized by a narrow gap in support for the contending candidates.[5] This is suggested by relevant survey data. For example, in one national poll conducted with regard to the 1988 election respondents were asked whether economic, social, or foreign policy issues were most important to their decision (table 4.1). Although foreign affairs came in last of the three, 10 percent of the respondents nevertheless considered it the most important issue. This, along with the portion of the electorate that would consider external relations as important as the other two classes of issues, suggests that foreign policy cannot be ignored in an election where the gap in the candidates' apparent support is not particularly large. Given the slim margin of the popular vote by which many presidential elections are decided, the risks of ignoring the possible electoral consequences of foreign policy can be substantial.

TABLE 4.1
*The Impact of Issue Categories
on Voting Intentions*

Type of Issue	Percent of Respondents Who Considered an Issue the Most Important
Economic	55
Social	13
Foreign Affairs	10
All Equally Important	13
Don't Know/No Opinion	1

SOURCE: Media General/Associated Press, 1988.

Similarly, in a survey of the voters of North Carolina (presumably not a state where international relations are deemed unusually salient), respondents were asked to rate the importance of foreign policy to their voting decisions on a scale of one to ten. As is apparent in figure 4.1, a considerable majority rated foreign policy on the upper end on the scale of importance.

At first blush, foreign policy would appear to have electoral consequences only inasmuch as issues matter; but this is not necessarily the case, for international affairs can influence the outcome of presidential elections in two ways. To begin with, even if voters are not much concerned with the specifics of the issues, a candidate's *image*, defined in such general terms as "competence," "leadership"—even "likability"—may be shaped by foreign policy positions. In turn, this will affect his or her electoral prospects, regardless of voter feelings about the substantive merits of the candidate's policy stances (which voters might not be in a position to evaluate anyway). This should be considered an *indirect* effect of foreign policy on electoral outcomes, for it operates through the image rather than substance of policy. Beyond that, a few issues do matter to the average citizen— to the extent that a candidate's stand on such issues will affect his or her prospects on election day. When this is the case, foreign policy may be said to have a *direct* effect on presidential elections.

The Indirect Effect

A close look at the public's evaluation of its three most recent presidents—Jimmy Carter, Ronald Reagan, and George Bush—suggests

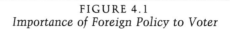

FIGURE 4.1
Importance of Foreign Policy to Voter

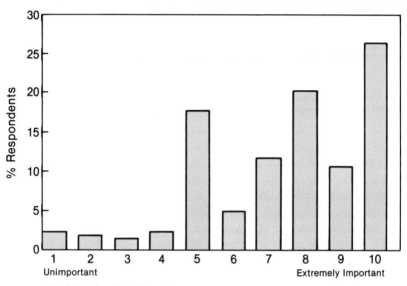

SOURCE: North Carolina State University

that the opinion in which a president is held, and consequently his image, depends on external as well as domestic performance. Since the latter part of the 1970s the Harris Survey and the Gallup Poll have regularly surveyed the public's general reaction to the way their presidents were handling the job. The public's opinion of their leaders' economic performance and handling of foreign policy was also polled. These three series of observations provide a picture of how the public's approval of economic and foreign policy is linked to its overall feelings toward the president.

Examining the patterns made by these three measures reveals that a president's overall popularity moves in rough tandem with public reaction to his handling of both foreign affairs and domestic economics. The relation between public endorsement of foreign policy and overall popularity is easily apparent, although it seems to have been particularly strong in Ronald Reagan's case. Consequently, the evidence provides preliminary grounds for believing that a president who cares about his overall image cannot afford an unfavorable

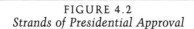

FIGURE 4.2
Strands of Presidential Approval

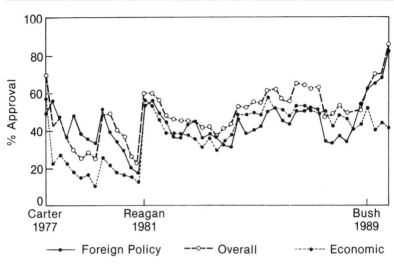

SOURCE: Gallup Poll and Harris Survey

impression of his foreign policy stewardship. A more adequate statistical test can also be applied. Formally expressed, the causal model we assume to be operating is the following:

Incumbent's percent approval$_t$ = α + β_1 {approval of foreign policy}$_t$
+ β_2 {approval of economic performance}$_t$
+ β_3 {identity of incumbent president}$_t$
+ v_t

The third variable (identity of the president) is coded to reflect which of the incumbents (Carter, Reagan, or Bush) is being examined, the purpose being to control for idiosyncratic personality characteristics associated with individual presidents that influence their overall popularity. Table 4.2 displays the results of a statistical estimation of the parameters and the predictive power of this simple model.

The $\hat{\beta}$s demonstrate how great an impact foreign policy and economic performance have on overall approval (formally, how much of a change in the latter is produced by a unit change in each of the former). The t statistics indicate how much faith we can have in these coefficients, while R^2 furnishes a measure of the model's overall predictive power. As the Durbin-Watson statistic (DW = 1.1) provided considerable grounds for assuming first-order autocorrelation of the residuals, the model was ultimately estimated by generalized least squares. The results are presented in table 4.2.

The model has considerable predictive power given the magnitude of $R^2(=0.90)$. Most interesting, the regression coefficient for foreign policy approval is significant at just about any conventionally accepted level (and almost equal to the coefficient for economic approval). Its magnitude $(\hat{\beta}_1 = 0.52)$ suggests that foreign policy creates an impact on overall presidential approval that is only slightly less powerful than the impact produced by voters' appraisal of his economic performance (a shift in foreign policy approval of approximately 2 percent would induce a change in overall approval of about 1 percent; a comparable shift in economic performance evaluation would be associated with a virtually identical change in overall approval). Interestingly, the identity of the incumbent had no statistically significant independent effect on his general approval rating. In a situation of volatile but not vastly different candidate approval ratings, no prudent contender for office could afford to ignore public responses to his or her foreign policy stances. Much as it is in an incumbent's interest to have a widely approved foreign policy, it is in a challenger's interest to discredit that policy in order to tarnish the incumbent's image. Indirectly then, foreign policy seems to affect electoral outcomes and, unless rather unrealistic assumptions are made about the motives of politicians, the conduct of foreign policy will be tailored around its domestic-political as well as international consequences.

TABLE 4.2
Presidential Popularity in Relation to
Economic and Foreign Policy Performance

Variable	Coefficient	t
Foreign policy approval	$\hat{\beta}_1 = 0.52$	6.7
Economic approval	$\hat{\beta}_2 = 0.54$	7.5
Identity of president	$\hat{\beta}_3 = 1.36$	0.64

$R^2 = 0.90$ $\alpha = 3.9$ N = 49

It is not entirely clear just *how* foreign policy behavior affects a candidate's image, but the general outlines are discernible. As long as a candidate's positions are within bounds considered acceptable by the political culture, the quality most desired by the public is that of "leadership," usually defined as firmness and decisiveness.[6] According to Robert Strauss, one of the deans of U.S. party politics, "If the electorate does not always understand the nuances of a foreign policy issue, it can readily sense a candidate's ability to deal with a difficult situation, project command bearing, and articulate a sense of national purpose."[7] As an illustration, it is not evident that the public preferred the specific substance of Ronald Reagan's foreign policy to Walter Mondale's; in fact, most Americans felt that Mondale would be better for peace. Nevertheless, most Americans seemed to feel that of the two men Reagan conveyed a much clearer sense of national purpose—as reflected in the significant majorities who thought that Reagan would do better at "increasing respect for the United States overseas" and "making people proud to be Americans."[8] As personality characteristics produce little independent effect, foreign policy evaluation seems to capture much of the impression of leadership generated by the incumbent.

Thus, as long as he or she remains within the mainstream of U.S. political culture, the firmness of a candidate's position on a few salient foreign policy issues may have a greater impact on the electorate than the actual substance of that position. By registering in the public's overall approval of the candidate, this impact is indirect; but we have said that foreign policy may occasionally produce electoral consequences of a more direct sort as well, and at times the specifics of an issue have mattered independently of, or in addition to, its impact on a contender's image.

The Direct Effects

The issues that most concern the electorate vary with changing international conditions, and there has been some evolution in public concerns over the past several decades. The debate between isolationism and internationalism, dominant during the earlier decades of the century and shortly after World War II, no longer has much meaning for a nation firmly committed to an active world role. On the other hand, the issue of America's Soviet policy did inject itself into most presidential elections of the postwar period—a reflection of the nation's concern with its principal rival for global supremacy. We will address the relation between electoral politics and attitudes toward the USSR in greater detail presently, but certain things must be noted at the outset.

Compared to the late forties and early fifties public perceptions of the Soviet Union had mellowed considerably by the 1970s, and the average American was no longer comfortable with the level of anti-Soviet rhetoric and militancy that seemed appropriate at one time. During the coldest years of the Cold War no greater anathema could be hurled at rival candidates for office than the charge of being "soft on Communism," and all candidates generally competed for the forefront of the political hardline on East-West matters.[9] But with the thawing of superpower relations, demonic conceptions of the Soviet Union became progressively more muted. This is not to say that superpower hostility abruptly receded from the domestic political horizon; an abiding dislike and distrust of Russia, coupled with a more inchoate fear of letting relations deteriorate too far, colored the rhetoric and probably the outcome of several presidential campaigns in recent decades. Nevertheless, relations improved visibly in the Gorbachev era, and a number of other foreign policy issues now compete for political attention as well.

To begin with, armed involvements abroad affect the average U.S. citizen sufficiently to have a significant effect on his or her voting decision. Although military interventions generate an initial upsurge in presidential popularity, this "rally-round-the-flag" effect dissipates soon after the costs of the intervention come to be felt. Accordingly, presidential candidates benefit from a perception that they will be in a position to bring the conflict to an earlier end than their opponents. For example, in August 1952 67 percent of those surveyed thought that Eisenhower would do a better job than Stevenson of handling the situation in Korea, while only 9 percent thought that Stevenson would do a better job[10]—and it is generally agreed that this affected the outcome of that year's election.[11] Similarly, in September 1972 58 percent of the public thought that Richard Nixon would deal better with America's Vietnam imbroglio, while less than half that number judged that George McGovern would be more effective.[12] Like Eisenhower, Nixon won by a large margin. Observers have pointed out that, despite Vietnam's salience at the time, the issue did little to affect the outcome of the 1968 presidential election.[13] But this is probably because the public failed to see a meaningful difference between Nixon's and Humphrey's Vietnam policies.[14] It is also worth noting that in 1971 more than twice as many Americans said that they would vote for a candidate who favored removing all U.S. forces from Vietnam than for one who would leave a residual force to assist the South Vietnamese.[15]

Thus, the prospect of seeing an end to an extended military involvement might sway a significant number of votes at election time. In a related vein, it is also recognized that Barry Goldwater's decisive defeat in 1964 had much to do with the public's fear of the consequences that his victory might have for peace and U.S. military involvements abroad.[16]

At least one other issue with foreign policy implications can influence the voting decisions of Americans, though the effect may not be quite as direct as with Soviet policy or military interventions abroad. We know that economic conditions exert a major impact on electoral outcomes.[17] As these conditions have become closely linked to the international economy, it is inevitable that an administration's foreign economic policies should affect its domestic political fortunes. After his defeat to John Kennedy in 1960 Richard Nixon claimed that his own purism on free trade lost him that close election. During the 1988 presidential campaign Michael Dukakis sought to portray Vice-President Bush as "soft" on foreign trade. As a *New York Times* headline recently observed, "When Running for President It's Hard to Be Free on Trade."[18] America's progressive drift toward protectionism during the past two decades bears testimony to the anticipated electoral costs of unfettered foreign competition. However, the link between policies and votes is somewhat circuitous here, for although voters react to objective economic conditions (e.g., rising unemployment), they are not always able to grasp the direct implications of specific foreign economic policies. A reaction to the occasional consequences of free trade, rather than an understanding of its actual mechanisms, is what probably affects votes.

There are, therefore, substantial grounds for believing that a candidate's stance on international affairs will influence his or her electoral prospects. Under the circumstances, it is no surprise that foreign policy may be twisted to conform to estimates of short term political

benefits rather than national need. A look at the record suggests that
this is indeed the case.

Politics and Foreign Policy

Before the twentieth century external affairs and domestic politics
were but loosely and sporadically linked—as with the disagreements
between Federalists and Democratic Republicans regarding the merits
of friendship with England or France. The first major intrusion of
partisan politics into foreign policy concerned U.S. adherence to the
Treaty of Versailles. Although this was partly a "turf" struggle between the executive and legislative branch, it was also a contest between Republicans and Democrats—the former flocking to the isolationism of Senator Henry Cabot Lodge, the latter generally loyal
to President Wilson's vision of collective security.[19] Even after Wilson
failed to secure Senate ratification of the treaty, the new Democratic
presidential and vice-presidential candidates, James C. Cox and Franklin D. Roosevelt, unsuccessfully sought to turn the 1920 election
into a "great and solemn referendum" on U.S. membership in the
League of Nations.[20] Whatever may explain the political interests and
passions that attended the politicization of the Treaty of Versailles,
the debate was soon submerged in political rhetoric and electoral
ambition, making a rational examination of its implications for the
U.S. national interest virtually impossible. Ultimately, United States
absence from the proposed system of collective security weakened
the Western democracies' ability to thwart the aggressive designs of
Germany, Italy, and Japan. In this manner, it contributed to the
breakdown of the international order devised at Versailles.

More recent examples of the enmeshing of foreign policy with
domestic politics abound, although some are not immediately apparent. The Cuban Missile Crisis is often remembered as President
Kennedy's finest hour, when through the bold management of threats
and power, he forced the Kremlin to back down from its attempt to
deploy medium-range nuclear forces within quick reach of the United
States. His skill and decisiveness produced the desired result, but they
were as much the product of domestic political need as of international calculations. In the weeks before the missiles were discovered,
numerous conservatives had complained of threatening Soviet moves

in Cuba, and congressional Republicans had warned that Cuba would be "the dominant issue of the 1962 campaign."[21] The president undoubtedly recognized his party's vulnerability in the midterm election and, as a member of his entourage explained, "the political needs of the Kennedy administration urged it to take almost any risk to get them out."[22] Even former President Eisenhower observed that "Kennedy might be playing politics with Cuba on the eve of Congressional elections."[23]

Possibly no episode in America's postwar history divided the nation as deeply as its involvement in Vietnam, but the war's course was largely driven by domestic politics. Although President Kennedy took the first military steps in Vietnam, his White House chief of staff, Kenneth O'Donnell, reported that the president quickly realized the costs of further intervention outweighed the anticipated benefits and that a pullout was desirable. But, as Kennedy admitted to Senator Mike Mansfield, "I can't do it until 1965." Apparently he felt "that if he announced a total withdrawal of American military personnel from Vietnam before the 1964 election, there would be a wild outcry against returning him to the Presidency for a second term."[24] In the event, America's ensnarement in Vietnam extended considerably past the point at which Kennedy hoped to bring U.S. troops home, and as the second half of the decade got underway public support for the war eroded. One week before the 1968 election, in a transparently political move designed to bolster Hubert Humphrey's faltering candidacy, President Johnson ordered a halt to the bombings. Nevertheless, the public may have been more impressed with Richard Nixon's claim that he had a "secret plan" to end the war honorably, and the 1968 election put an end to the Democrats' eight-year hold on the presidency.

His secret plans notwithstanding, President Nixon continued American involvement in Vietnam through his entire first term, and this came to include military incursions into neighboring Cambodia. But by the time of his 1972 reelection bid Nixon used public revelations of peace initiatives and Kissinger's announcement that "peace is at hand" to strengthen his electoral prospects.

Despite his slowness at extricating the United States from Southeast Asia, Nixon is rightly credited with major foreign policy achievements, but many of them had domestic political roots. With regard to detente and the opening to China, it has been suggested that "their timing and handling smacked heavily of political calculation."[25] Nevertheless, these initiatives helped undermine George McGovern's attempts to base his electoral appeal on the image of a "peace candidate," and they contributed to Nixon's resounding victory at the polls.

More recently still, the latter years of President Carter's term in office were marked by his inability to disentangle his own political fortunes from foreign policy. The plight of the American hostages in Teheran dominated the political agenda in 1980, and Carter initially tried to exploit this issue to his electoral advantage. The "Rose Garden" strategy, by which he cloaked himself in an aura of nonpartisan leadership by refusing to debate Senator Edward Kennedy during the presidential primaries, as well as his misleading claim on the morning of the Wisconsin primary that a breakthrough regarding the hostages was imminent, bore the marks of politics rather than of statesmanship. Ultimately of course, his failure to secure their release contributed to his political undoing. At the same time, the increase in Soviet assertiveness during the late seventies, and especially the invasion of Afghanistan, made it politically imperative that Carter move away from his initial efforts to salvage detente—a retreat that he undertook with vigorous dispatch.

The enmeshing of foreign policy with domestic political expediency may be lamentable, since the conduct of external relations becomes delinked from objective international conditions, but it is hardly surprising. Although democracies differ somewhat in this respect, competitive politics generally blocks the segregation of the internal and external realms. Leaders have sometimes tried to transcend short-term political concerns, but failures outnumber successes.

Harry S Truman is remembered as a leader who managed to rise above partisan politics when major matters of state were at issue. It is reported that, when a friendly congressman asked how the U.S. assistance program to Greece and Turkey might affect the Democratic party's political fortunes, Truman turned "in cold anger" on the hapless congressman. "In these matters I never want to hear that damn word politics mentioned again," the president declared.[26] Nevertheless, he readily used Cold War themes to undermine his domestic political challengers—most notably former Vice President Henry Wallace, who had been pressing for a more accommodating stance toward Moscow—during the 1948 election campaign.[27]

Mirroring Truman, President-elect Reagan warned his cabinet members never to be influenced by political considerations. "I don't want anyone ever to bring up the political ramifications of an act," he told them. "The decision should be based on what's good for the nation, not what's politically beneficial."[28] Lofty sentiments notwithstanding, the reality of electoral politics caught up with this President as well. By the spring of 1981 political pressure from American farmers, and the prospect of their electoral impact in 1982, led him to lift the grain embargo that Jimmy Carter had imposed against the USSR after its invasion of Afghanistan. This despite Russian pressure on Poland and notwithstanding the administration's insistence that U.S. allies withhold various industrial products from the Soviets. During his first term in office, the President also dispatched a large contingent of U.S. marines to Lebanon, in what was broadly defined as a "peacekeeping" mission. Even after 241 Marines were killed in a terrorist attack in October 1983, Reagan lambasted his Democratic critics in Congress for suggesting that the U.S. troops should be withdrawn, contrasting his critics' readiness to "surrender" with his own more determined attitude. But with an upcoming election, "Reagan's political advisers felt the Marines had to be removed to defuse the issue in the 1984 Presidential campaign."[29] Accordingly, and while criticizing Democrats for advocating withdrawal, Reagan quietly authorized plans to remove the troops in February 1984.

Not every foreign policy act is guided by an estimate of electoral advantage. President Carter's decision to cede control of the Panama Canal to the Republic of Panama was, by all indications, based on principle alone, and taken despite expectations of considerable domestic criticism. Truman's resolution to fire General Douglas MacArthur, despite the public adulation in which the World War II hero was held, was politically risky and rooted solely in a judgment of what the national interest demanded. Still, we should not lose sight of the more general pattern. There are exceptions to most rules, but recent history suggests that this is precisely what they are and that, very frequently, presidential candidates bend foreign policy to their own political calculus. The authors of one much-quoted study of the domestic context of foreign policy observed that, "we have become all too accustomed to giving our partisan struggles priority over consistency and coherence in our foreign policies."[30] Former Secretary of State Alexander Haig complained that the White House has succumbed to "the impulse to view the presidency as a public relations opportunity and to regard Government as a campaign for reelection."[31] The criticism may be substantially valid, but electoral democracy makes it difficult for politics to stop at the water's edge, and the question is not just whether statesmanship can rise above electoral calculations when foreign policy interests are at stake, but what the consequences of an inability to do so may be.

Foreign Policy Consequences

The entangling of external affairs with domestic politics carries consequences of two major sorts, both of which suggest that policy is partially disconnected from the international circumstances to which, in principle, it should be responsive. To begin with, politicization creates jarring *discontinuities* in the conduct of external affairs, which is often shaped around a domestic electoral cycle rather than the nature of foreign challenges. Further, it has probably led to an unnecessarily *combative* posture, having made it especially difficult to set relations with the Communist world on a nonhostile footing.

Foreign Policy Discontinuity and the Impact of Electoral Cycle

The record indicates that foreign policy is subjected to rhythms and periodicities linked to electoral cycles, which, having no logical connection to external needs, sometimes impairs its effectiveness at dealing with both friends and rivals.

Discontinuity Assuming that national interests are fairly stable, the conduct of external affairs should, in principle, be approximately as predictable as the international environment. Yet the path of U.S. foreign policy has been more jagged than international circumstances would justify, and some of its major lurches have been associated with presidential elections and transitions from one administration to another. Since there is no reason to think that either the national interest or the state of the world changes radically at such times, domestic political calculations appear to have determined the course of external relations at critical junctures in American history. As a result, foreign policy's grounding in international circumstances is weakened, impairing its coherence and sense of direction.

Arms control bears heavily on the national interest, yet it has been buffeted by an electoral logic more powerfully than other facets of external policy. Eager to create self-serving contrasts, presidential candidates typically draw sharp distinctions between their views of national security and arms control and the views of their political rivals. The factual and logical foundations of their positions are generally less important than the boldness of their stance and its ability to play upon the public's assumed concerns. Upon stepping into office, victors are thus bound by campaign promises that may not reflect credible national needs.

President Kennedy's dramatic denunciation of a missile gap to the disadvantage of the United States was proven wrong soon after he came to office, but the surge in America's intercontinental missile force prompted by his charge assumed its own momentum and was not reversed when the mistake was acknowledged. It took a full decade before strategic arms limitation negotiations got fully underway again, and a SALT I agreement was not signed before 1972. SALT II talks were launched soon thereafter, but they too were quickly derailed. Jimmy Carter had campaigned on a new approach to arms control and, shortly after entering the White House, he abandoned the incremental character of the SALT negotiations, which sought to deal even-handedly with the weapons of greatest concern to each superpower, in favor of sweeping reductions in those strategic systems in which the Soviet advantage was most pronounced. His proposals, carried to Moscow in March 1977, called for a comprehensive reduction in land-based missiles, including a 50 percent cut in the Soviet Union's heavy SS-18 missiles. As these were the mainstay of the Russian arsenal, and since few proposals were made regarding submarine-based missiles (the central pillar of the U.S. arsenal), the Russians indignantly dismissed the proposal. The administration was left to pick up the pieces and attempt to get arms control started again. Finally, in June 1979 a SALT II treaty was signed, but with the Soviet invasion of Afghanistan and another election underway it was never ratified by the U.S. Senate.

Having denounced SALT II as "fatally flawed" during the campaign and having implied that most existing arms control agreements served Soviet designs rather than U.S. interests, Ronald Reagan's approach to arms control was to abandon it altogether. "The argument," he announced, "if ever there is one, will be over which weapons [to build], not whether we should forsake weaponry for treaties and agreements."[32] When the first U.S. proposals were made in 1982 they seemed designed primarily to be rejected by Moscow, and it was not until the president's second term in office that serious negotiations got underway once again. By that time, however, each side had made considerable new investments in military growth, and increasingly ambitious proposals were required to put a meaningful dent in nuclear arsenals.

Discontinuities induced by presidential elections and transitions have affected other aspects of U.S. foreign policy as well. President Eisenhower's relative indifference to the Third World was replaced by President Kennedy's virtual obsession with it as an arena of East-West conflict. Soon after the new administration stepped into office, the focus on Europe in the fifties was balanced by concern with the possible Soviet penetration of developing nations and the need to combat left-wing wars of "national liberation." The Bay of Pigs invasion and the first steps toward military involvement in Vietnam were products of this shift in foreign policy emphasis. The Carter administration's step-by-step efforts to fashion a Middle East settlement addressing the concerns that separated Israel and its Arab neighbors was dropped in the Reagan administration's unsuccessful attempt to sweep regional differences under the rug and to create an anti-Soviet military alliance of "pro-Western" states in the region.

Whereas the Nixon and Ford administrations' pragmatic approach to geopolitics left little room for concern with human rights, President Carter, in a pronounced departure from realpolitik, initially made this a cornerstone of his foreign policy, targeting abuses by both Cold War rivals and right-wing friends. During the 1980 campaign the Reagan camp denounced this policy as one undermining regimes, their unsavory domestic politics notwithstanding, that supported America's geopolitical interests. With Ronald Reagan's election human rights was transformed from a general national concern to a propaganda weapon tailored to Cold War objectives. The Bush administration's approach to human rights has proven rather close to that of the Nixon and Ford presidencies.

Thus, it appears that elections and presidential transitions, often more than international circumstances, have accounted for the frequent volatility in U.S. foreign policy. A major result has been to make it harder for both friends and rivals to develop a predictable working relationship with the United States. Alliances are less stable when they are buffeted by electorally-induced shifts in the senior partner's positions, for other members no longer know quite what to expect from their leader, and the organization's priorities and strategies become uncertain. Helmut Schmidt, for example, complained that "as Chancellor, I worked under four presidents, and its quite an experience, I can tell you. . . . First Carter sent his vice- president to tell us almost everything done by his predecessors was wrong. Then along comes Reagan and tells us the same thing."[33]

By the same token, it is harder to moderate rivalries when one side's attitudes toward the other are not primarily governed by the other's behavior. Rivalries that do not terminate in a clear-cut victory by one side are usually ended through a process of progressive mutual adaptation—by learning which activities are rewarded and which are punished and by adjusting behavior accordingly.

Robert Axelrod, for example, has demonstrated that the most effective method by which cooperation evolves from adversarial relations is by a strategy of tit-for-tat responses, wherein each side responds in kind to the other's actions while taking care never to overreact or to initiate hostile behavior.[34] However, this assumes that behavior on both sides is not driven by conditions stemming from internal sources that bear little objective relation to the other's actions. In other words, nations can only evolve a cooperative pattern of behavior toward former rivals if they know what behavior on the rival's part their own initiatives will engender. But if that rival's behavior is largely driven by a domestic logic, such understanding is much harder to achieve.

Electoral Cycles Often the electorally induced policy shifts do not last very long, as the pressure of international reality and the pull of the center in U.S. politics eventually correct the excesses produced at times of intense foreign policy politicization. Even so, external affairs are subjected to a rhythm and periodicity during the typical electoral cycle that bear no compelling relation to the nation's international needs. As Zbigniew Brzezinski has explained, "Every Administration goes through a period of ecstatic emancipation from the past, then a discovery of continuity, finally a growing preoccupation with Presidential reelection."[35] One consequence is a significant reduction of the time during which a president may pursue an effective foreign policy—especially during his first term in office. Another is a domestically propelled, but from the perspective of national needs arbitrary, alteration of periods of assertiveness and reticence in conduct of external affairs.

Quite apart from the fact that U.S. presidents sometimes come to office with no significant foreign policy experience and founder during their first year for lack of accumulated wisdom, often they are also constrained by campaign promises made primarily for electoral purposes. Thus, the early phases of many presidential administrations are frequently marred by a combination of ineptitude and excess. Consider Kennedy's Bay of Pigs fiasco and his inglorious performance at the Vienna summit with Khrushchev, Jimmy Carter's unproductive focus on human rights (alienating both friends and rivals), Reagan's maladroit policies in the Middle East and Western Europe as well as his shrill and sterile anti-Sovietism.

By the fourth year of their first term most presidents are preoccupied with fending off electoral challenges. Not only can they devote less attention to foreign affairs but, when they do, they are once again tempted to tailor policies to their own political purposes rather than to long-term national needs. As William Quandt, a former National Security Council official, has observed, presidential approaches to foreign policy undergo significant shifts over their first four years in office.[36] Much as presidents tend to be overly bold during their first year in the White House, they are likely to be obsessed with avoiding major foreign policy failures as the reelection campaign looms ahead. As a result, they frequently become prudent to the point of inaction during their fourth year. For example, fear of alienating the nation's conservatives at the time of his 1976 reelection campaign led President Ford to abandon further efforts on behalf of detente and SALT II. In a similar vein, President Reagan's fear of being saddled with a foreign policy failure in 1984 led to his hasty retreat from Lebanon in February of that year. Alternatively, presidents may simply adhere to formulas of behavior that seemed to work to their advantage in the past (e.g., an increased emphasis on a favorable military balance vis à vis the Soviet Union), neglecting the specifics of current challenges.

With the first year often written off to inexperience as well as to the impact of campaign-related claims and promises, and with domestic politics again ascendant during the fourth year, only two years may be available for the display of true foreign policy statesmanship over the typical first term. For example, it was during the two middle years that President Carter engineered the Camp David accord and completed the arms control negotiations that led to the SALT II treaty. Kennedy's first major steps toward arms control with the Soviet Union were taken in his third year in office. Similarly, Ronald Reagan made the first serious efforts at getting along with Moscow during the second and third years of his first term. In May 1982 he called upon the Kremlin to join the United States in what came to be known as the Strategic Arms Reduction Talks (START) and, despite a few rhetorical flourishes in 1983, grain sales were liberalized, the administration ended its ban on furnishing gas pipeline equipment to Russia, and arms control negotiations in Geneva began to show the first signs of activity. President Bush outlined a strategic arms control agreement with Moscow in the second year of his presidency and signed a treaty on chemical weapons as well.

However, since foreign policy initiatives do not often produce immediate results, even activities undertaken during the second year may bear no fruit until the third. Consequently, it may be that the most active and successful period in a typical president's first term will be his third year. A rough quantitative check of the record supports this notion. For example, if we examine the chronology of arms control activity during presidential first terms before the (as yet not completed) Bush first term, noting the times in which agreements with the Soviet Union were reached, we find that not a single treaty was signed during the first year or second year, and only one, the SALT I treaty (composed of the ABM treaty and the Interim Offensive Arms Agreement) during the fourth year (1972). By contrast, fully eight treaties were signed during the third year. The second year of the Bush administration witnessed some progress on arms control, but the final version of a strategic accord awaited his third year in office.

U.S.-Soviet summit meetings, which overlap partially with the signing of arms control agreements, reveal a similar, if somewhat less

TABLE 4.3
Arms Control Treaties and the First-Term Cycle*

First Year		Total = 0
Second Year		Total = 0
Third Year	Partial Test Ban (1963)	
	Hotline (1963)	
	Outer Space (1967)	
	Peaceful Nuclear Explosion (1976)	
	Seabed (1971)	
	Accident Measures (1971)	
	Hot Line Modernization (1971)	
	SALT II (1979)	Total = 8
Fourth Year	SALT I (1972)	Total = 1

*Included are those significant arms control agreements that were principally or exclusively bilateral agreements between the United States and the Soviet Union. The Table does not include President Bush's first term, as it has not been completed at the time of writing. Since most of the relevant preparatory work was concluded before President Nixon's resignation, the 1974 Vladivostok meeting is attributed to his second term in office.

TABLE 4.4
U.S.-Soviet Summit Meetings and the First Term Cycle*

First Year	Kennedy-Khrushchev 1961 (Vienna)	Total = 1
Second Year		Total = 0
Third Year	Eisenhower-Khrushchev 1955 (Geneva)	
	Johnson-Kosygin 1967 (Glassboro)	
	Carter-Brezhnev 1979 (Vienna)	Total = 3
Fourth Year	Nixon-Brezhnev 1972 (Moscow)	Total = 1

*Does not include President Bush's first term (as yet not completed). As most of the relevant preparatory work was done before his resignation, the 1974 Vladivostok meeting is attributed to President Nixon's second term.

stark pattern. For completed first-term cycles a single meeting took place both during the initial year of a president's first term in office (1961) and during a fourth year (1972). However, fully four took place during the third year (1955, 1967, 1974, 1979). President Bush had one summit meeting during his first year, two during his second year, and, if our hypothesis holds,and if the pattern applies to the post-Cold War era, should have at least two summits and achieve major arms control goals during his third year.

Plainly, there are exceptions to this four-year rhythm. President Nixon traveled to China and signed the SALT I agreement during the fourth year of his first term. Also, some of Lyndon Johnson's most ill-advised escalatory moves in Vietnam occurred during his second and third years in office. Counterexamples notwithstanding, the general pattern cannot be overlooked, nor can its consequence of reducing the period in which effective foreign policy is conducted during the typical presidential first term to approximately two years.

One might reason that, during his second term, a president's foreign policies should be free from the political pressures of his first term. We saw that President Kennedy planned to scale back the U.S. military presence in Vietnam if he were returned to office a second time. Richard Nixon ultimately did withdraw American troops after he was reelected in 1972. In the same vein, each of Ronald Reagan's five summits with Mikhail Gorbachev occurred during his second term. The problem with a second term is that during its last two years—and certainly during its fourth year—the administration's "lame duck" status inhibits major new policy initiatives. On the one hand, the imminence of another election suggests that many of the incumbent's policies will be challenged and that the constituencies on which his policy support rested during previous years may come apart. Moreover, foreign governments understand from experience that a new administration does not feel bound by its predecessors' commitments, and they may deem it wiser to postpone major undertakings with the United States until after a new leader is elected.

Even before the U-2 incident decisively ended the "spirit of Camp David," it had become clear that not many new foreign policy initiatives were to be expected from Eisenhower. As Townsend Hoopes has pointed out, by 1960 "the Eisenhower administration ran steadily down like a tired clock, its energies spent, its coherence blurred."[37] Moreover, Khrushchev's willingness to scuttle the Paris Summit was probably facilitated by his realization that not much was to be expected of a president in his final months in office. Despite his popularity, Ronald Reagan, America's only other postwar president to serve two full terms, could not complete strategic arms reduction talks with the Soviet Union in 1988—despite earlier predictions to the contrary and despite his ability to negotiate the relatively "easier" agreement on medium-range missiles in Europe a year earlier. By 1988, too, his administration's efforts to secure a Middle East settlement had come to a virtual halt.

These, then, are effects linked to the pressures of competitive domestic politics. Their consequences include abrupt discontinuities and periodicities in foreign policy that affect both its coherence and consistency. They reduce by approximately one half the period of time during which a president can conduct foreign policy on the basis of objective national needs rather than short-term electoral calculations. They produce boldness and reticence at times when international conditions may call for the opposite. Although these effects concern the style and timing more than the *content* of foreign policy, the pressures of electoral politics have also had a systematic impact on the actual substance of America's external affairs—encouraging certain types of behavior while discouraging others. We have already suggested that domestic politics and protectionism in foreign economic policy go hand-in-hand. It is perhaps more important, and almost certainly less well understood, that election campaigns have had predictable, and probably harmful, consequences for the tone of East-West relations.[38]

East-West Relations, National Security, and Electoral Politics

Since the beginnings of the Cold War domestic politics have more often led to a hardening of U.S. stances toward the Soviet Union, and to an increase in U.S.-Soviet tension, than to improved prospects for superpower accommodation. Presidential elections in particular have often been associated with a sharpening of Cold War rhetoric and a strengthened commitment to military growth. Moreover, social psychologists have reported that rhetoric directed toward the Soviet Union has traditionally experienced declining "complexity," becoming more rigid and simplistic at election time.[39] While several national elections have had no discernible impact on East-West relations, it is difficult to claim that any (with the possible exception of 1972) has actually led to a more conciliatory attitude toward Moscow. Reagan's decision to terminate the grain embargo against Russia in 1982 was probably taken with a view to the electoral impact of farming states on the midterm elections, but even this was accompanied by unusually harsh anti-Soviet rhetoric and vastly upgraded strategic efforts.

The link between elections and hardened anti-Soviet stances dates back to the Cold War's early years and has been rooted in expectations of where the greatest electoral rewards lie. In his bid for a second term in 1948, President Truman heeded Clark Clifford, his close political adviser, who had pointed out a year before, when Truman

lagged in most public opinion polls, that "there is considerable political advantage to the Administration in its battle with the Kremlin. . . . The worse matters get, up to a fairly certain point—real danger
of imminent war—the more there is a sense of crisis. In times of crisis
the American citizen tends to back up his President."[40] Truman's
drumming on Cold War themes and his attacks on the relative dov-
ishness of his challenger, former vice-president Henry Wallace, il-
lustrated the point.

The presidential contest of 1952, which pitted Dwight Eisenhower
against Adlai Stevenson, was substantially dominated by East-West
issues. Rifts in strategies for dealing with Moscow developed at the
outset of the campaign and were, it seems in retrospect, as closely
linked to electoral ambition as to authentic policy differences. Already
at the Republican national convention in Chicago, General Douglas
MacArthur had lambasted the Democrats as "those reckless men"
who "set the stage for Soviet ascendancy and our own relative decline," a statement rewarded with a seven-minute ovation. At the
same convention, former President Herbert Hoover spent more than
one hour castigating the Democrats for their Soviet policy.[41] John
Foster Dulles, as the campaign's chief foreign policy spokesman and
strategist, made denunciations of Truman's foreign policy a central
theme of Eisenhower's campaign.

But it was not obvious why this should have been so. Truman had
been closely associated with the doctrine of containment and had
taken a very firm stance toward the Kremlin. In fact, there is little
evidence that Eisenhower had serious problems with his predecessor's
foreign policy, for he had entered the campaign largely in opposition
to the isolationism of Senator Robert A. Taft (the Republican party's
most likely nominee had Eisenhower not entered the primaries).[42]
Still, as historian John Lewis Gaddis has pointed out, "presidents are
rarely made by endorsing their predecessors . . . and Eisenhower
quickly came under pressure to put 'distance' between himself and
the incumbent administration in the area of foreign affairs."[43]

The Eisenhower campaign sought to create this distance, not only
by castigating Truman for insufficient anti-Soviet assertiveness but
by making the improbable though electorally rewarding claim that
the Republicans, unlike the Democrats, would not be content to
contain the USSR, but would actually roll back its influence to secure
the liberation of Eastern Europe. Electoral calculations were probably

closely connected to these claims. Gaddis has concluded that they were "motivated . . . far more by determination to lure East European voting blocs away from the Democrats than from any realistic expectation of 'rolling back' Moscow's sphere of influence."[44] Eisenhower won the election and, predictably enough, did little to modify Truman's containment policy—although we must assume that the Republican campaign rhetoric did much to heighten the security fears of a Soviet regime that had, in any case, determined that the West yearned mightily for its demise.

The 1956 election was marked by the unusually mild manner in which each side dealt with the other's foreign policy positions. Unrest in Poland, the Soviet invasion of Hungary, and the Suez crisis generated a temporary upsurge in bipartisanship, and a thorough politicization of foreign policy was deferred until the election of 1960— when it emerged with a vengeance. John F. Kennedy's campaign is remembered for his hammering on the theme of a "missile gap" to America's disadvantage, one that the Republicans had allowed to develop and that he, with greater determination and concern for the nation's security, would be sure to close. The issue may have accounted for his victory (which was in any case razor thin), but shortly after his election it was revealed that any missile gap as such decisively favored the United States.[45]

Broad foreign policy issues were once again tethered to electoral ambition in 1976. During the Republican primaries, Ronald Reagan led an assault on détente, declaring that "there is little doubt in my mind that the Soviet Union will not stop taking advantage of detente until it sees that the American people have elected a new President and appointed a new Secretary of State."[46] As an act of political prudence, President Ford decided to place some distance between himself and the conciliatory East-West policies of previous years, and he announced that the word *détente* would be purged from his vocabulary.

Superpower relations further deteriorated in 1980, and Ronald Reagan, who had rather effortlessly secured his party's nomination, denounced Carter's Soviet policy as one that, "bordering on appeasement," had encouraged the Soviet invasion of Afghanistan and could even be inviting another world war.[47] "They were right," he declared. "The Soviet Union has bet that Mr. Carter is too weak to respond to the invasion of Afghanistan. And they were right."[48] The Republican platform, in a departure from Nixon's and Kissinger's stress on "essential equivalence" as a U.S. strategic posture, demanded the pursuit of military *superiority* over the Russians.

Despite the substantial mellowing of U.S.-Soviet relations during the second part of the decade, the 1988 election quickly assumed a traditional flavor. Democratic nominee Michael Dukakis sought initially to capitalize on what he felt was a softening national mood in response to improved East-West relations, and he argued against major new weapons systems and foreign policy intervention but, adhering to tested formulas, George Bush moved the debate onto more traditional ground—defending each of these strategic weapons and going so far as to question Dukakis's patriotism. President Reagan jumped into the fray as well. When he vetoed the proposed military budget on grounds of its alleged insufficiency in August 1988, at a time when the presidential election had begun acquiring momentum, Senator Lloyd Bentsen, the Democrats' vice-presidential nominee, accused the president of "poisoning defense politics with partisan politics," complaining, "Decisions on national defense are now being based on the latest political poll at the White House."[49]

The sharpened tone of East-West relations that so often accompanies U.S. presidential elections and the impetus it frequently imparts to the arms race had a predictable impact on the Soviet Union's behavior, tilting its own foreign policy positions in a confrontational direction. In 1960, for example, the outlook was reasonably good for a significant improvement in U.S.-Soviet relations. Following his removal of the hardliners of the "anti-party" group in June 1957, Khrushchev emerged as the undisputed leader of the Soviet Union—with a penchant for domestic reform and for a relaxation of East-West tension. Moreover, his 1959 visit to the United States and the spirit of Camp David that it produced portended well for future cooperation—and even for modest progress toward arms control.

The U-2 incident of May 1960 was an obvious blow to hopes of improved relations, but these were further undermined by the anti-Soviet campaign rhetoric of the Kennedy-Nixon presidential race and by the sharp increase in U.S. military programs following Kennedy's campaign promises. This in turn caused Khrushchev to abandon his plans for a significant troop reduction intended to divert resources toward domestic programs.[50] Similarly, the conservative challenge launched by Ronald Reagan against President Ford in the 1976 primary elections, much of which focused on assaults against his Soviet policy, led Ford to abandon not only his references to détente but also his attempts to reach a SALT II agreement with Moscow before the election. As he pointed out, with an approaching election, "it would be impossible to discuss SALT II in a rational way."[51]

Although the Soviet Union's international conduct must bear its share of the onus for the deterioration of East-West relations in the late seventies, the collapse of détente was also a product of the Kremlin's decreased estimate of its benefits—largely because of the opposition of U.S. congressional hardliners to commercial concessions for Russia. Also, by the end of the decade it had become unlikely that the SALT II treaty, which had been signed in June 1979, would manage to garner the two-thirds majority needed for its ratification by the Senate. This realization probably removed, from Moscow's point of view, some of the disincentives that might have made its adventurism in the Third World—and ultimately its invasion of Afghanistan—less probable.

Why has domestic political competition tended to drive America's Soviet policy toward confrontation rather than cooperation? Is it because as political contenders reach more deeply into the ranks of the public for votes at election time they find themselves addressing a segment of American society with scant formal education, an above-average level of chauvinism, and a greater gut-level adherence to military power and anticommunist rhetoric? In the words of one observer, "The policy preferences of these temporarily politicized citizens differs from those of the more attentive public. . . . They are quicker to oppose arms control. Their customary foreign policy preference is parochial nationalism that expresses itself either in isolationism or in jingoism."[52] According to this view, then, leaders find it most politically rewarding to stress confrontational and anti-Soviet themes at election time.

To some extent this is plausible, but the explanation must be qualified. It is true that the less educated segments of American society have tended to be more suspicious of other nations and less likely to endorse conciliatory policies toward the Soviet Union. To illustrate this point table 4.5 displays the percentage of respondents to a national survey expressing some level of approval of the Soviet Union, both overall and at various levels of education. The results are displayed for 1972, a year when détente was near its peak; for 1982, a period when superpower relations had deteriorated to their lowest level in several decades; and for 1989, when relations were again on the mend. On each occasion, those with a college education were likely to feel less hostile to the USSR than those with no more than a high school education, and the latter, in turn, were less likely to have negative feelings about Russia than those with a mere grade school education.

Nevertheless, an adequate explanation of the link between elections and anti-Soviet stances is more complex. To begin with, although the less educated may be especially likely to oppose conciliatory policies, they are also generally less likely to vote than those with more formal education—a factor that somewhat offsets the politician's incentive to tailor foreign policy stands around their concerns and preferences.[53] More important—and until well into the Gorbachev era—levels of public approval of the Soviet Union have been low at *every* educational level. For example, even in 1972 only about one-half of the *college-educated* public expressed any approval of Russia, and overall this amounted to just 40 percent of the public. Thus, even during the best of times, the modal national feeling toward the Soviet Union, not just that of its less educated segment, has been quite negative.

The more general explanation for the link between partisan competition and confrontational East-West postures is rooted in the *political reward structure* that has traditionally characterized American democracy and has come fully into play at election time. The point is that, from the perspective of the electorate, a U.S. leader's Soviet policies could err in two ways. The first type of error consists in a mistaken *underestimate* of the threat posed by the USSR and a consequent insufficient response to that threat (e.g., through a failure to

TABLE 4.5
Approval of the Soviet Union by Levels of Formal Education

	1972	1982	1989
Overall national	40%	21%	66%
College education	54%	26%	70%
High school education	37%	19%	64%
Grade school education	32%	16%	48%

SOURCE: The Gallup Poll

take adequate military measures). The second consists in a mistaken *overestimate* of the Soviet threat and a subsequent overreaction to Moscow's pronouncements and behavior, which leads to the heightening of East-West tension and the undertaking of defense programs that later prove to have been unnecessary.

As there has almost always been some ambiguity about Russia's capabilities and intentions, political leaders have faced the prospect of making either sort of mistake. Accordingly, a rational leader would estimate which of the two could engender greater political punishment and would lean toward the type of error apt to be less costly. What has tilted the U.S. reward structure in a confrontational direction is that the electoral punishment for a mistaken underestimate of the Soviet challenge (associated with an underreaction to that challenge) has typically been greater than the punishment associated with a misguided overestimate of the threat (and a consequent overreaction). Because of this, the traditionally preferred response of both incumbents and challengers was to stress pugnacity over cooperation and military strength over negotiated arms control. Having labored the point elsewhere,[54] I will not address the roots of this biased political reward structure here. The main point is that, over the past several decades, it has nudged policy in a confrontational direction at election time—when the principal rewards and punishments provided by the political system are meted out. The end of the Cold War may modify the specifics of the political reward structure as it concerns the Soviet Union, but whatever its modified form, it will continue to influence foreign policy—especially during election years.

The domestic political correlates of international behavior have not yet been the objects of extensive examination. Nevertheless, in addition to whatever this chapter may have suggested, available research buttresses the suspicion that electoral pressures tend to disassociate foreign policy from the international conditions to which it is supposedly the response. Heightened external combativeness around election time has been a specific manifestation of the more general trend. For instance, one study detected a tendency for force to be invoked more frequently when elections were imminent.[55] Another found that during both the Korean and Vietnam wars U.S. presidents were especially likely to escalate the use of force if they were seeking reelection at the time.[56] Similarly, Philip Tetlock has found that American leadership postures toward the Soviet Union become more simplistic at election time.[57] In a major overview of the electoral correlates of national security policy Bruce Russett concluded that "if toughness is more likely than conciliation to glean electoral rewards, a president who is aware of this can be expected to tailor his foreign policy accordingly. Apparently most are, and do."[58]

Caveats on Political Competition

The conclusions thus far have not been heartening, but they may have been somewhat one-sided. Concerned with the undesirable consequences of electoral democracy for the conduct of external affairs, we may have neglected a number of benefits that, wholly or partially, could offset these liabilities. In fact, elections and the political circumstances that surround them could enhance the wisdom of policy in a variety of ways, mitigating the undesirable side-effects they also produce. To begin with, the exchange of ideas and the scrutiny to which policies are subjected at election time could ensure their examination from more than one angle, making it likely that glaring inconsistencies or untruths would be exposed. This could compensate for some of the problems I have mentioned and, on many occasions, make policy wiser than it would otherwise have been. In addition, competitive democracy makes it likely that the most abject foreign policy failures will not go unpunished on election day and, consequently, that the political interests of leaders will not be as much divorced from those of the nation as the preceding analysis implied. These are important considerations and, if valid, they suggest a more complex picture than the one thus far presented.

In an article entitled "What's Right with U.S. Campaigns," Robert Strauss noted that election campaigning "enriches the country's understanding of candidates and their leadership abilities . . . educates the American people about serious foreign policy choices to a degree that may not be possible at other times, and . . . can help Americans discover where they want to go as a nation."[59]

The virtue of campaigns, according to Strauss, is that issues receive their "most sustained and thorough airing," while the "electorate's receptivity to new ideas peaks." In addition, candidates are "matched against the foreign policy demands of the office," providing the voter with an opportunity to gauge not only the merits of foreign policy proposals but also the leadership abilities of those who will be charged with their implementation. The prospect is that foreign policy will be wiser and more effective as a result. However, what is theoretically possible may escape actual practice.

At the margin, of course, particularly egregious foreign policy errors are apt to succumb to democratic scrutiny; although the worst excesses are likely to be avoided, lesser problems may be exacerbated by electoral rhetoric and campaign-generated policies. Issues may be obfuscated rather than clarified, candidates' positions may be misleading rather than enlightening, and the level of debate may not be conducive to public education. Even Strauss recognizes that "the first serious concern of any serious candidate is not public education but getting elected"[60]—and the latter concern has almost certainly dominated the former. The desire to score quick political points against an opponent by stoking popular anxieties, by presenting self-servingly distorted views of international reality, and by reinterpreting opponents' positions with little regard for their actual content, is a permanent possibility at election time. Under the circumstances, debate does not necessarily produce the educational benefits that electoral competition could theoretically provide.

Eisenhower and Dulles's claim during the 1952 campaign that they would not stop at the mere containment of Communism but, through their greater determination, would actually force its *rollback* ran counter to any reasonable notion of what was feasible. It is hard to believe that the Republican campaign took its own rhetoric seriously and, once elected, the new administration did little to deliver on its promise. Conceivably, the major impact of its election-related rhetoric was to intensify Russia's and China's qualms about the United States, while the American public was uncertain as to what it could expect from its government. John F. Kennedy's 1960 theme of a missile gap (for which the Republicans were held responsible) had, as was later demonstrated, no basis in military fact, yet it provided a major impetus to the race in intercontinental nuclear missiles.

Similarly, Ronald Reagan's insistence in 1980 that the nation faced a "window of vulnerability" (for which the Democrats were said to be responsible) led to a major strategic buildup and a temporary abandonment of arms control. Yet the president's own Commission on Strategic Forces concluded three years later, as should have been obvious all along, that no such window existed.[61] In 1964 Lyndon Johnson misled the public about his intentions regarding Vietnam. Barry Goldwater, the Republicans' nominee for the presidency, pressed his "Let's Win" policy of total victory and called for a blanket bombing of Vietnam. Adopting a moderate stance, Johnson promised in September that "we're not going north and drop bombs at this stage of the game," because, as a responsible leader, he had "to think about the consequences of getting American boys into a war with 700 million Chinese."[62] Five months later he ordered the first U.S. bombing raids on North Vietnam.

It is important that, on the evidence examined in this book, public opinion is not *naturally* predisposed to embrace the sort of rhetoric by which candidates for political office seek to sway it. This raises an apparent paradox. On the one hand, the public appears not to be afflicted by the whimsical and extremist propensities with which it is often charged; on the other hand, by politicizing foreign policy issues at election time, office seekers and their support groups seem to assume that the electorate will respond favorably to themes associated with emotiveness and intemperance. Though seemingly paradoxical, this need not imply irrationality on the candidates' part. It is unlikely that they so misunderstand the public as to present issues in a manner that will damage their own electoral prospects, but they may be responding to other features of political, and especially, electoral, logic. If, as I have argued, public opinion on international issues is relatively stable, it is difficult for a politician to derive much electoral benefit by adopting a significantly differentiated stand in this area. Yet the need to distinguish their positions from those of their opponents is powerfully felt, particularly by challengers. Accordingly, to create a new constituency on international issues to which a candidate can appeal with his or her own specific views, it is necessary to jog some portion of the public out of its stable groove of opinion. This is most effectively done by creating a sense of *crisis* in external affairs, to which established modes of thinking no longer seem appropriate and within which the candidate's stance is presented as the appropriate response. As V. O. Key observed, "Presidential leadership seems most effective in the activation of latent opinion when a sense of threat, frustration, or deprivation is widely felt within the population."[63]

It is at this point that the public's modest store of factual knowledge begins to matter, for the sense of crisis (due, for instance, to a newly discovered Soviet threat) is generally conveyed by invoking "new" factual information (e.g., on an emerging "window of vulnerability"). Lacking an independent store of information against which to evaluate such claims, the public is malleable. Left to its own reasoning and predispositions, it might not adopt views generated for electoral purposes; yet its slim factual knowledge makes it more responsive than it otherwise might be to a rhetoric designed to produce a sense of foreign policy drama.

Despite significant evidence of campaign-induced derailment from above, an important point should not be ignored. As I have already suggested, even if electoral politics exact a toll on the continuity and wisdom of U.S. foreign policy, democratic political competition nevertheless provides some insurance against the most egregious excesses, and it often encourages the correction of many of the problems it is inclined to create.

When foreign policy violates the limits of what interests, culture, and expectations have defined as acceptable, when its actual or potential costs are too great, or when it flies in the face of the most elementary common sense, it will eventually be pounced upon by the opposition and, sooner or later, denounced by the electorate. Under such circumstances, information previously unknown will often be forced upon the national consciousness and myth-making will encounter far greater obstacles than when policy remains within the bounds deemed acceptable by traditional practice and routine public forbearance. The U.S. involvement in Vietnam approached a situation of this sort. Not only did it raise a number of ethical quandaries that Americans had not previously faced, it also violated acceptable cost-benefit calculations in foreign affairs. The costs of the war were greater than could be justified without invoking major national values and interests, but few Americans believed that these were truly at stake. Accordingly, opposition to the war did emerge, and although it originated outside the electoral context in the hearings of Senator Fulbright's Senate Foreign Relations Committee, it found its way into the elections of 1968 and 1972. The challenges to U.S. policy in Vietnam ultimately crystallized in the process of domestic political competition that, in turn, expedited the nation's decision to remove itself from this distant conflict.

But, if U.S. democracy usually manages to avoid mistakes involving great departures from established policy practice and expectations, it is less obviously suited to dealing with cumulative distortions that are often closely linked to electoral competition. Thus, a tension of sorts characterizes American democracy. On the one hand, the need to justify policy at election time places an outer limit on excesses and mistakes. On the other hand, election-related competition makes certain mistakes more probable. The consequence is that both the remedy and the malady are stimulated simultaneously—and the point of equilibrium between these opposing drives is but dimly perceived. However one conceives the problem the solution may be very difficult. Not only are the stakes very large for the participants in electoral competition, but the currency with which the electoral game is played does not require a very firm backing—as long as most players agree to accept this fact. John Burnheim may be right in maintaining that "overwhelming pressures to lie, to pretend, to conceal, to denigrate or sanctify are always present when the object to be sold is intangible and its properties unverifiable until long after the time when the decision to buy can be reversed."[64] Because of this,

> sound strategy demands that in bidding for votes one pays as little as possible in clear commitments and plays down any unpopular aspects of policies one is committed to. Usually, it pays the opposition more to concentrate on spinning their own deceptive webs than on attempting to pin their opponents down. They fear being pinned down themselves. It is safer to stick to slogans and empty rhetoric, or to play on people's fears and prejudices. It pays to fight myth with myth.[65]

What is generally true of electoral politics may apply with particular force to matters of foreign policy—since the nature of the good is even harder to identify and circumscribe than with regard to domestic policy. At the same time, the lack of a domestic constituency whose interests are directly linked to external affairs (unlike the case of, say, agricultural or educational policy), and the feeble store of factual information that the average citizen can claim, make it less likely that the myths will be subjected to the cold light of self-interested scrutiny and exposed by those outside the electoral arena whose fortunes it adversely affects. In any case, the problem is much more closely tied to incentives operating at the pinnacle of the political pyramid than to deficiencies at its base. In all likelihood, too, it is reinforced by the conviction that, in matters of external relations, the public should rarely be given credit for adequate judgment and awareness of its own. The paradox is then the following: the more firmly one espouses realpolitik's standards of good foreign policy, the greater the grounds for concern with the consequences of its view of where the major locus of foreign policy wisdom lies.

Chapter 5

DEMOCRACY AND DECEPTION

*Without publicity, no good is permanent; under
the auspices of publicity, no evil can continue.*
—Jeremy Bentham

Subterfuge in international relations is generally viewed with easy
indulgence. Chicanery toward enemies and rivals is more typically
applauded than censured, while deception of friends and allies is often
considered a necessary evil in a context of hard-nosed realpolitik. The
greatest normative quandaries surround *domestically* directed deception which, when associated with foreign policy, is often justified
by the need to shield policy from the consequences of disruption
from below. As such, domestic deception flows from a conviction
about the main source of friction between democracy and the effective
conduct of external affairs.

In previous chapters I argued against the assumption that the greatest domestic threats to foreign policy originate within the body of
society; and I could find little to support the belief that impulses at
the pinnacle of the political system are more conducive to wisdom
in the management of international affairs. Conceivably, however,
there are recesses of policy where these conclusions do not apply,
and where there are sound reasons for keeping the people uninformed.

The Scope of Deception

Woodrow Wilson's admonition that government should be "all out-side and no inside" has never adequately characterized U.S. external affairs.[1] Only in secret session was Congress informed of the controversial Jay Treaty with Britain (though the news was soon leaked to the newspapers). The circumstances of General Jackson's incursion into Spanish Florida were shrouded in subterfuge. In 1844, in an attempt to avoid public debate on the issues, the Tyler administration tried to slip a treaty on the annexation of Texas through the Senate in executive session. Franklin D. Roosevelt was less than open with the American people on his intentions concerning U.S. participation in the war in Europe. The deficient probity and candor of the Johnson, Nixon, and Reagan administrations' foreign policy has been amply recorded and discussed.

The study of deception comprises the examination of several forms of dissimulative behavior, the most common variant being simple secrecy—suppressing from democratic debate information on matters of substantive or procedural significance. From the rarely contentious cases of military and intelligence secrets, the practice becomes more controversial as it shades into less obviously sensitive areas of foreign policy.[2] A particularly encompassing variant involves government's unwillingness to disclose not only certain of its activities but the broad policies with which it has associated itself. Lyndon Johnson's initial unwillingness to admit the extent of his plans for escalating American involvement in Vietnam reflected a readiness to conceal his true purpose from the nation—as did, several decades earlier, Franklin D. Roosevelt's pretense of contemplating no direct American involvement in World War II.

A form of dissimulation with particularly significant implications for popular control of government reaches beyond the methods and the substance of policy to shield the very *locus* of policymaking from public view. This practice was taken to particular lengths in the Iran-Contra affair, when not only was the considerable autonomy vested in a narrow portion of the National Security Council staff concealed from almost everyone not directly involved in the operation but also parts of the foreign policymaking machinery were located outside the government itself—the process of funding for the Contras, which Congress had tightly controlled, having been partially transferred to *private* bodies not subject to democratic accountability.[3]

One might wish to distinguish the withholding of information
(secrecy) from the conscious purveying of falsehood (lying). Although
less opprobrium usually attaches to the former, the two often share
similar practical implications. To begin with, there are times when
the consequences of secrecy may be as harmful as those of lying, for
the implications of societal ignorance may be comparable in both
cases.[4] Further, secrecy and lying are not causally unrelated. Much
as lying implies a certain amount of clandestinity, so secrets often
beget lies—refusing to divulge the truth, one generally is impelled to
offer an alternative.[5] For example, since U.S. efforts to encourage the
coup that ousted South Vietnam's Ngo Dinh Diem in 1963 were part
of an unacknowledged policy, the administration was forced to deny
the role it played in this regard.[6] As then-U.S. ambassador to Saigon
Henry Cabot Lodge subsequently maintained, "We never participated
in the planning. We never gave any advice. We had nothing whatever
to do with it."[7] On another occasion, in mid-November 1986, President Reagan told the nation, "We did not, repeat, did not trade
weapons or anything else for hostages."[8] A statement equally un-
truthfully adjusted to claim that "the modest deliveries, taken together, could easily fit into a single cargo plane."[9]

Thus, the respective consequences of the two forms of deception
may not be as different as the stigma respectively attached to each
would suggest. Because of the extent to which they are usually entangled, both secrecy and lying will be encompassed by the notion
of *deception* in this chapter; they will be relegated to separate categories only when there is evident reason for doing so.

The National Interest and the Suspension
of Accountability

Secrecy and departures from complete truthfulness (white lies) play
an accepted, and in many instances useful, role in relations among
individuals, with respect to such needs as tension reduction, face-
saving, the avoidance of minor inequities, and so forth.[10] A similar
departure from ethical absolutism applies to political life as well.
While governmental openness to scrutiny is a measure of democracy,
absolute candor is not one of its prerequisites, and few argue that a
society's interests are best served if nothing is ever withheld from

those outside the councils of government. Plato's concept of the "noble lie" assumed the occasional need for benevolent deception by leaders of those whom they lead, to the latter's ultimate advantage.[11] And Erasmus once observed that the people must sometimes be misled: "For the crass multitude there is a need of temporary promises, figures, allegories, parables . . . so that little by little they might advance to loftier things."[12]

Consequently, the notion that people may have to be lied to for their own good is not new, and, although contemporary thinking generally views so paternalistic a perspective with disfavor, acceptable limits to truthfulness sometimes can be found. Depending on one's outlook, these may do no more than accommodate the need to keep sensitive military secrets from potential adversaries, or they may encompass the confidentiality of governmental deliberations, much of foreign affairs, and, at the margin, even the substance of national policy. The *Federalist*, for example, found justification for executive secrecy on matters of diplomacy (where "perfect *secrecy* and immediate *despatch* are sometimes required") and in the "business of intelligence" (which demands that "the persons possessing it can be relieved of the apprehensions of discovery"). One might then argue, along with many utilitarians, that the justifiability of any act must be evaluated in terms of its consequences and that, by weighing the relative implications of candor and deception in the conduct of foreign policy, the balance may sometimes vindicate the latter.

Democracy does not require that Americans should be aware of everything their government is doing, if for no other reason than because this is not what they themselves would rationally desire. The acquisition of any information involves a cost—at least in terms of the opportunity costs of other activities foregone in the process of obtaining it. Under the circumstances citizens would not rationally seek information unless the expected benefits of each additional piece of knowledge were at least equal to the cost of acquiring it.[13] Since, moreover, people rarely establish a link between foreign affairs and their personal welfare, little effort is normally made to seek relevant information—a conclusion sustained by the scant factual knowledge that most Americans were shown to have on international affairs (chapter 2).

Still, the point should not be taken too far. Certain types of foreign policy decisions have so substantial an impact on the concerns of citizens that they do expect relevant information will not be kept

from them—for example, information concerning military entangle-
ments, matters of direct economic import to some segments of society, or issues that strike close to the heart of the average American's
conception of what is right and proper. In any case, one should not
confound the issue of citizen interest in acquiring information with
governmental willingness to provide it. It is not a condition of liberal
democracy that people always inform themselves of what their government is doing, but the willingness of leaders to provide that knowledge generally is. In other words, the public's frequent indifference
to information does not, in itself, justify a lack of government candor.

Despite its potential benefits, then, deception does some violence
to democratic principle, especially to the principle of the political
accountability of government.[14] Governmental activities that are not
fully disclosed can be neither adequately rewarded nor censured by
the democratic process. Deception makes it difficult to know who
should be called to account for decisions and conduct. Policies that
are the product of debates and reasoning inaccessible to the public
and its immediate representatives may be too easily presented for
approval in either/or terms, foreclosing necessary qualifications.[15]
Much as the existence of market oligopoly in an economy depends
on some level of consumer ignorance,[16] so the concentration of executive power is related to its capacity for secrecy and dissimulation.

Where the risks are recognized, the justification for governmental
dissimulation is generally found in the concept of *reason of state*:
the idea that an interest transcending that of society's component
parts is embodied in the State which, because of this, is not subject
to the standards of behavior to which individuals are normally held.
Reason of state is related to Machiavelli's admonition that a Prince
must "learn how not to be good,"[17] and to the associated notion of
arcana imperii—the "mysteries" or secrets of state that are intrinsic
to its elevated nature and autonomous morality.

Nevertheless, because deception undermines democratic accountability, very substantial benefits to the State must be claimed if it is
to be vindicated, and two grounds for justification are generally offered. First, that sensitive information acquired by American citizens
may also come into the hands of hostile foreigners, to the detriment
of national security. Second, that Americans, if told certain things,
might impede their leaders from doing what the latter alone understand to be in the country's best interests. Plainly, the latter argument

touches the substance of my discussion more directly than the first. But, if the second argument more closely involves the consequences of democracy for foreign policy, both concern the consequences of foreign affairs for democracy. Under the circumstances, both must be addressed.

Deceiving Americans with Foreigners in Mind

Deceiving Americans as the price of misleading adversaries and enemies is most often justified by the claims of national security: because the persistence of democracy depends on it, democracy sometimes must bear the short-term costs of its own long-term survival. In a speech to the American Newspaper Publishers Association, President Kennedy admonished journalists not to ask, "Is it news?" but rather, "Is it in the interests of national security?"[18] On the occasion of signing the Freedom of Information Act in 1967, Lyndon Johnson, who had never been very enthusiastic about it, professed to have "always believed that freedom of information is so vital that *only national security*, not the desires of public officials and private citizens, should determine when it must be restricted"(emphasis added).[19] A former assistant secretary of defense for public affairs explained that, when national security is at stake, the government has the right, "indeed the duty" to lie.[20]

At the height of the Pentagon Papers controversy, William B. Macomber, Jr., deputy undersecretary of state, argued the government's position as it sought to suppress the papers' publication by the media. "Perhaps if we could talk only to the American people," he explained, "we could tell a lot of secrets, but there is no way you can talk only to the American people. Other people listen in."[21] Macomber's point is sometimes valid, but the question is how far it should be taken, and the pitfalls of taking it too far became evident in the context of national defense. Military secrets are the most widely accepted category of information that must be kept from adversaries, but even in the realm of weaponry and force posture it is better to make some things known to one's enemies. For example, if deterrence is the purpose of armed force, it is important that actual or potential enemies should appreciate the extent of one's military might. Moreover, an insufficient understanding of a rival's military capacity often leads

to worst case assumptions on this score—causing each side to seek
more military power than it objectively requires, and generating levels
of tension that might have been avoided had each side known more
about the other's actual strength. Commenting on the U.S. missile
buildup of the early sixties, which was subsequently shown not to
have been justified by the Soviet Union's strategic programs, Secretary
of Defense Robert McNamara explained that

> since we could not be certain of Soviet intentions, since we could
> not be sure that they would not undertake a massive buildup, we
> had to ensure against such an eventuality by undertaking a massive
> buildup of our own Minuteman and Polaris forces. . . . But the
> blunt fact remains that if we had had more accurate information
> about planned Soviet strategic forces, we simply would not have
> needed to build as large a nuclear arsenal as we have today.[22]

Intelligence activities and capabilities bear heavily on national defense as well, and the need to protect sources of covertly obtained,
yet crucially important, information is widely accepted. Nevertheless,
if exaggerated perceptions of a rival's strengths and predatory intentions are to be avoided, each side should appreciate the other's ability
to find out enough about its own plans and capacity. Thus, while
certain information must be kept from hostile foreigners, there seems
to be no direct correlation between national security and the withholding or distortion of information, even on military and intelligence matters.

In addition, and beyond a narrow core of generally accepted meaning, national security may be too amorphous a notion to provide
clear guidelines for justifiable domestic deception.[23] For example, the
concept may be limited to matters dealing with national *defense*—
specifically, the ability to deter aggression or to repel it should deterrence fail. This is the thrust of the definition of national security
presented by Gabriel Almond, who considers it the business of "the
allocation of resources for the production, deployment, and employ-
ment of what we might call the coercive facilities which a nation
uses in pursuing its interests."[24] Slightly broader is the conception
offered by former Secretary of Defense Harold Brown, who describes
national security as "the ability to preserve the nation's physical integrity and territory; to maintain its economic relations with the rest
of the world on reasonable terms; to protect its nature, institutions,
and governance from disruption from outside; and to control its

borders."[25] Defined in such terms, some role for deception, even of one's own people, generally would be accepted. But the concept has also been defined to include virtually all of international affairs. For example, Richard Allen, former White House national security adviser, maintained that the term "must include virtually every facet of international activity, including (but not limited to) foreign affairs, defense, intelligence, research and development policy, outer space, international economic and trade policy, monetary policy, and reaching deeply even into the domains of the Departments of Commerce and Agriculture. In a word, 'national security' must reflect the presidential perspective, of which diplomacy is but a single componeny."[26]

So expansive a conception of national security as a basis for legitimate deception would leave virtually no room for accountability in foreign affairs; yet the boundaries of the concept are not demarcated by a generally accepted body of meaning. Although one respected legal scholar urged, in the wake of the Nixon presidency, that Congress "take appropriate action to clarify the meaning of 'national security,' establish its legitimate uses, and promulgate guidelines for future applications,"[27] its intrinsic elusiveness makes it an unsuitable candidate for precise definition.

In any case, it is doubtful whether executive invocation of national security should suffice to designate a matter as one justifying secrecy or other forms of dissimulation. In one of the most widely publicized instances of this sort, the Nixon administration took legal action to block the media from publishing the Pentagon Papers. Though it repeatedly claimed that "the nation's security will suffer immediate and irreparable harm,"[28] unless publication were halted, no discernible damage to national security was caused by the government's inability to prevail in the matter. The presence of the Castro regime had been branded a threat to national security during the Kennedy and Johnson presidencies, yet the United States has weathered its presence with no major damage for several decades. Every military system requested of Congress has been justified as crucial to some facet of national security, yet there has never been a perceptible increase in the country's vulnerability from refusals to fund specific requests or from a system's technological demise.

As one departs from the narrow core of *defense*, it becomes less and less clear what national security benefits of deception justify its cost in terms of political accountability, for as one moves beyond the need to protect against military attack, the concept of security becomes subject to increasingly subjective and potentially controversial interpretations (see chapter 6).

Even if one could agree on the circumstances in which information should be kept from Americans to mislead hostile foreigners, the issue of legitimate deception would not be resolved, since so many cases of secrecy and prevarication have no apparent roots in needs of this sort. The secrecy surrounding the Reagan administration's attempts to trade arms for hostages with Iran cannot be explained by a wish to mislead foreigners (the relevant foreigners obviously knew about it). Whatever one might think of the rationale for President Nixon's clandestine bombings of Cambodia in 1970, his attempts to mislead Americans on this score had little to do with deceiving adversaries (the bombing was no secret to the Vietcong, to the North Vietnamese, or to any of their allies). When President Kennedy initially concealed, in October 1962, the discovery of Soviet missiles in Cuba, it was plainly not with the aim of hiding their presence from the Soviet Union.

If many instances of deception cannot be and are not justified by the need to fool the nation's foreign adversaries, the circumstances of legitimate deception are not thereby exhausted. It may be argued that there are occasions when information should be kept from Americans even when it is available to hostile foreigners—an argument substantially rooted in fears of disruption from below.

Deceiving Americans In Their Own Best Interest

Although deception of the public based on its own assumed interests carries a heavy dose of paternalism, observers might consider similar practices justified at other levels of social intercourse. A doctor, desiring to steer a patient away from an unhealthy practice (e.g., alcohol abuse) might feel justified in overstating the health risks involved. Fearing that an unexpected plunge in the stock market might, by generating investor panic, feed upon itself, respected financial analysts may misleadingly minimize the implications of the drop in the interests of the investors themselves.

Paternalistic deception may have a valid role to play in political life as well. In matters of state policy it is sometimes claimed that

Americans must be deceived (even if enemies are not) because, otherwise, government would be hindered by its public from doing that which it recognizes to be in the public's best interest. In other words, and in an argument for governmental autonomy rarely made with regard to purely domestic affairs, government leaders should not subject policy to disruption from below, which would follow if certain forms of information came to the attention of a citizenry not capable of grasping its implications. Morgenthau, for instance, explained that, if U.S. leaders are not to sacrifice good policy to public opinion, they must, "by devious means gain popular support for policies whose true nature they conceal from the public."[29] No president of the United States, he complained, "is capable of translating his judgment and that of his advisers into action without overcoming great difficulties, running great risks, and resorting at times to evasion, subterfuge, and manipulation."[30]

A deception practiced for the national good and based on the assumption of deficiencies within the body of society is one with inherently flexible justificatory standards. It is not necessary that claims of national *security* be invoked—a broad conception of the national interest could suffice. For example, during a crisis in relations with another nation the government might wish to keep the true state of affairs from its public for fear that, driven more by emotion than by an adequate grasp of the implications of various courses of action, it could drive its leaders to precipitous, and possibly calamitous, action. Or else, not understanding the issues involved in important though complex negotiations, the public might misconstrue the rationale for certain compromises and punish its leaders from doing what the national interest objectively required.

We are not treading on virgin territory here, since such arguments invariably assume that, at some level of foreign policy awareness, the government's grasp of the issues is much better than the grasp of those to whom it is accountable. Relying, then, on the tripartite distinction between levels of understanding developed in previous chapters, we might begin by asking whether society's relative ignorance of *factual* knowledge justifies specific pieces of information being concealed from it. The explanation would be that, lacking an adequate backdrop of information against which to evaluate the facts withheld, the public or its immediate representatives might place a mistaken interpretation on these facts, leading them to force an inappropriate policy upon the better-informed leadership.

In principle, there may be instances when inadequate knowledge is more dangerous than no knowledge at all; as a practical matter, however, it is hard to find concrete and realistic examples when this is so.[31] A variant of the argument, according to which relative ignorance leads to emotionally driven behavioral extremes, is not much more convincing. To begin with, it seems a priori as likely that relative factual ignorance will induce prudence rather than intemperance (as, for example, generally seems to be the case with business decisions, particularly those involving financial outlays). Further, as chapter 2 sought to document, the evidence does not suggest that the public is driven by passion to immoderate positions.

Even if we grant that government is justified in worrying about the impact of the public's modest factual knowledge on important foreign policy decisions, it is hard to invoke many instances of governmental deception linked to anxiety on this particular score. More plausibly, government may worry that the *contextual beliefs* or *normative convictions* of many Americans are incompatible with the policy it deems necessary. For example, a popular uneasiness at dealing with regimes linked to terrorism probably dissuaded President Reagan from revealing his policy of trading arms for hostages with Iran. Public and congressional resistance to widening the war in Indochina made it seem preferable to keep bombing raids of Cambodia secret from the nation. Popular and congressional unwillingness to deal with a government guilty of considerable violence against prodemocracy students probably caused the Bush administration to send a high-level mission to Beijing clandestinely, in what it viewed as an instance of sensible realpolitik.[32]

The proposition that government deception is necessary, not just because the citizenry or its legislature know less, but because their grasp of goals and causal connections is inferior, is not compelling. The only plausible grounds for believing this would be if, on certain sensitive matters of international policy, better factual information naturally led to superior awareness at one or both of the *other* two levels. But, for at least two reasons, this generally will not be the case. First, while the argument might apply to contextual awareness, it cannot credibly be stretched to cover normative judgments. Second, as I have argued, even on contextual matters there is generally a diminishing marginal benefit to increasingly detailed and specialized factual knowledge. Accordingly, the leap from factual information to overall judgment should not be made too hastily. As Nicholas Katzenbach, incumbent of a number of high-ranking foreign policy positions, observed, "The subtle insights of specialists or classified pieces of information are often accorded a totally undeserved attention and importance in comparison to some widely shared insights and knowledge."[33] Referring to the blurring of factual and more general knowledge, he complained of "a tendency to assume that such fundamentals as the amount of dollar cost the public will bear to reduce nuclear risks, or the loss of lives that we will bear to avoid a particularly offensive weapon, are technical decisions for experts— although these decisions involve only value judgments, not specialized knowledge, once the choices are fairly laid out."[34]

Other statesmen have concurred. Dean Rusk, secretary of state to both John F. Kennedy and Lyndon Johnson, was even more concise on the issue. Shortly after leaving office he observed that "I really do not know of any secrets which have a significant bearing upon the ability of the public to make their judgments about major issues of foreign policy."[35] Reflecting on the value of secret information to sensible decisions, Arthur Schlesinger, Jr., concluded that "the country would have been far better off during the Kennedy years had the White House confined itself to reading newspaper dispatches about Vietnam and never opened a Top Secret cable from Saigon."[36]

A different twist to the argument about inadequate popular awareness is provided by Samuel Huntington, who does not suggest that it is the public's factual ignorance or its penchant for emotional excess that hobbles political leaders' pursuit of desirable policies; rather, the problem is rooted in the national political culture, in an American credo that is both highly idealistic and congenitally opposed to the political authority that government requires if it is to do what its public expects of it. It follows that "secrecy is thus necessary to hide the facts of power, and deception is necessary to make those facts appear different from what they are. The latter is the natural extension of the former: secrecy is the shield of power and deception the cloak of secrecy."[37]

Although Huntington extends his argument to cover the institutions and conduct of foreign policy, it is difficult to feel convinced by his interpretation. His assertions are vigorously made, but little empirical evidence is ultimately provided to demonstrate the existence of this American credo. In the case of foreign policy, there has been no indication of public concern with the vast concentration of power in the hands of the national security bureaucracy. Although complaints sometimes flow from the pens of academics and editorial journalists, there has been little evidence of a *popular* outcry against strong government when it comes to external affairs. Congress has occasionally challenged the authority of the executive, but it appears to have been motivated by a concern with its own Constitutional prerogatives—and by a somewhat different set of foreign policy incentives—rather than by a sense of violated credo. In short, it is difficult to find a compelling justification, or a convincing explanation, for deception in the fact of an overly idealistic political culture wedded to the notion of weak government.

If one agrees that deception has less of a role to play than proponents and practitioners of *realpolitik* argue, there remain occasions when Americans should not be told (and may not wish to know) the whole truth—independently of the need to deceive hostile foreigners. At times of particularly acute international crisis even the slightest chance that public pressure would drive policy in the wrong direction may justify misleading public about the true state of affairs.

The Cuban Missile Crisis is the example that comes to mind most readily. Public feelings toward Fidel Castro had reached a state of such implacable hostility that immediate military action might have been forced upon President Kennedy had emotions been unleashed at the height of the crisis. Given the scope of the peril, it is hard to fault Kennedy and his advisers for keeping developments from the nation during the early stages of the crisis.

There are also matters that, while not encompassed by most definitions of national security, may nevertheless be incompatible with total openness. It is generally understood that deliberations within councils of government and other bodies must sometimes be secret if a candid exchange of views is to be ensured. For example, the internal deliberations of courts (especially juries) are generally kept secret by the judicial branch, and members of Congress preserve the confidentiality of communication with their staff. Even the Freedom of Information Act provides for exemptions for information "relating to inter- and intra-agency memoranda."

An obvious instance of deliberations conducted in secret that produced more than they might have otherwise was the Constitutional Convention of 1787. Among the rules adopted for the convention was the stipulation "that nothing spoken in the House be printed, or otherwise published, or communicated without leave."[38] The reason for secrecy was primarily to allow deliberation to take place without outside pressure. On less momentous occasions, deliberation might also benefit from concealment. In a book that finds few excuses for secrecy Sissela Bok observes that "if administrators had to do everything in the open, they might be forced to express only safe and uncontroversial views, and thus to bypass creative or still tentative ideas. As a result, they might end by assuming hasty and inadequate positions. Chances to learn might be lost; premature closure with respect to difficult issues would become more likely."[39]

In many instances, negotiations with foreign governments also demand secrecy if they are to yield meaningful fruit. Flexibility required by compromises may not be displayed if initial positions are made public, for they could be the objects of premature domestic politicization. From what we know of the role that foreign policy symbolism plays in competition for political office, the costs to policy can be substantial. Similarly, tentative and exploratory stances are harder to assume if they must immediately be subjected to public scrutiny. President Nixon was perhaps correct when he maintained in 1973 that, without secret negotiations, there would have been no rapprochement with China, no U.S.-Soviet summit, and no SALT I agreement.[40]

At the same time, secret policy deliberations and diplomatic negotiations generally exact the same toll on democratic practice that all governmental deception does. While one can consider ways of establishing trade-offs between practical exigencies and normative principles, one should also ask whether deception and democracy cannot, at times, actually be made compatible. This would require guidelines that, if followed, would indicate that the two do not clash. The most credible rule, I believe, rests on the principle of *prior assent*.

The Principle of Prior Assent

The terms of the principle are as follows: to ensure that the substance of democracy is respected in the presence of deception, the public from whom the truth is hidden in a specific instance should have agreed to be held, temporarily at least, ignorant in that *general* class of occurrences. Where this is the case, democratic consent can be said to have been given, and the incompatibility between democracy and foreign policy is removed.

Practical objections to the principle of prior assent can be raised, especially when it is taken to endorse prevarication rather than secrecy.[41] If, for example, the government were to make a statement or claim in an area in which it had received a mandate to lie, it would probably not be believed by whomever it sought to mislead—undermining the whole purpose of permitting the subterfuge. While problems may arise at the margins, our current purpose is to find a way of resolving the inconsistency between democracy and deception, and the concept of prior assent offers the most promising principle on which a resolution might stand.

Bok's argument that, with respect to lies justified as being for the public good, "only those deceptive practices which can be openly debated and consented to in advance are *justifiable* in a democracy,"[42] involves a standard that is somewhat more restrictive than our own. Still, it accords with the general thrust of our suggestion as long as the words "can be" are not taken to imply "have been," for the assent need not be a product of an explicit, "open" debate. In fact, it could be granted in at least two manners: (1) by assent of the legislature, or (2) by implied popular acquiescence.

Legislative Consent The legislative process provides the more obvious way in which democratic assent may be granted for deception. Agreeing that under some circumstances the national interest requires that certain information be kept from themselves and/or the public, legislators might determine, in accordance with the principle of checks and balances, acceptable conditions for doing so. In this manner, leadership could be authorized, even by explicit statute, to keep certain things secret from the nation, and no major injury would be done to democratic practice.

Thus, no matter what one might think of Great Britain's Official Secrets Act, possibly the most encompassing document of its kind in a democracy, it was bestowed on the government by the House of Commons, not by the government upon itself. In this regard, it is significant that the United States has no analogous piece of legislation, no comprehensive statute setting the boundaries of permissible domestic deception as the price of respect for political realism. The military establishment had historically maintained a rudimentary system of classification to protect sensitive military information but between the infamous Sedition Act of 1798 and the Cold War, classification was not the product of civilian authority and its scope did not go beyond information directly linked to the national defense. The Espionage Act of 1917 made it illegal to transmit military and cryptographic information abroad with "intent or reason to believe" that it would be used to America's detriment. However, this covered the transmittal of such information to enemies; it did not set the foundation for what could be kept secret from U.S. citizens. In 1940 President Roosevelt endorsed the system of military classification, but cited for this purpose only the flimsiest of legal justifications.

The 1947 National Security Act (which created the Central Intelligence Agency and the National Security Council) gave the Director of Central Intelligence authority for statutory secrecy by entrusting him with "protecting intelligence sources and methods from unauthorized disclosure." It also made the NSC responsible for recommending to the president ways of protecting sensitive information. Thus Congress recognized a need to shield some information related to national security from public view. But the question is how broad a legal basis for secrecy this provided, since it seems, from its context, that this piece of legislation was directly concerned with protecting information related to military matters and to intelligence, and that it applied only to agencies with such responsibilities. Certainly, there is no indication that it was designed to shield the *substance* of actual policy from democratic scrutiny.

When, for the first time in U.S. history, the security classification system was applied to agencies with neither military nor intelligence functions, this was accomplished by President Truman's Executive Order 10290 of September 1951, not by a legislative act. Although the lack of congressional challenge may be taken as tacit agreement with the president, it must be appreciated that this was the time of the Cold War's apotheosis and of rampant McCarthyism—a period of general conviction that the nation was locked in a struggle for survival with Communism and of the belief that a war between the superpowers was quite likely. To the extent that the context of agreement provides an interpretation of its intended substance, what tacit

concurrence there was logically referred to the world as it was perceived to be at that time, not to the broader gamut of possible international conditions.

In 1953 President Eisenhower's Executive Order 10501 mitigated
some of the more extreme provisions of the procedure instituted by
Truman (e.g., by narrowing the definition of classifiable material),
and John F. Kennedy instituted a process for automatically down-
grading security classifications and declassifying material whose revelation would no longer threaten national security. But a renewed
tightening of the classification system was instituted by President
Reagan, who discarded President Carter's stipulation that the benefits
of classification had to be weighed against the "public interest in
disclosure" and the requirement that classification be based on an
"identifiable" potential risk to national security should the information be disclosed.

Thus the scope and intensity of classification has generally been
the product of executive decision rather than legislative act. Admit-
tedly, Congress has occasionally legislated secrecy. One such instance
was the Atomic Energy Act of 1954, which subjected atomic energy
information to a system of security classification. Another was the
Case Act of 1972, which required that Congress be informed of all
executive agreements with foreign nations while it explicitly provided
that disclosure could be limited to members of the Senate Foreign
Affairs and House Foreign Relations Committees, under an injunction of secrecy, should the president determine that national security
so required. In both its 1966 and 1974 variants, the Freedom of
Information Act allowed an exemption for material that, pursuant
to a legitimate executive order, had been classified in the interests of
national defense and foreign policy. Nevertheless, this was clearly an
attempt to restrict the scope of unwarranted classification rather than
an endorsement of existing standards of secrecy. Much the same could
be said of legislative attempts to check the profusion of undisclosed
executive agreements with foreign nations. In most cases, Congress
has simply responded with apparent resignation to the political dictates of situations created by the executive.

One could point out that democratic consensus cannot be reduced
to *legislative* action (implying congressional supremacy, it would be
alien to the separation of powers). In particular, the tenet of *executive
privilege*, a principle with dubious constitutional roots but with a

long history of congressional and judiciary acquiescence, could provide the normative foundation for at least some portion of governmental dissembling. In this way it could also be argued that a basic
reason deception and democracy are not always incompatible is that
there exists an *implied* popular mandate granting the executive a
right to exercise a judicious amount of deception with regard to Americans in the national interest (even if this is not translated into statutory provisions).[43] The second condition for assuming prior assent
for domestically directed deception therefore rests on the belief that
there is evidence of a moral agreement between government and
governed on the circumstances justifying a lack of political openness.

Implied Popular Consent

The concept of implied consent permeates governmental thinking,
and it does have some intuitive foundation. The danger derives from
the fact that its exact boundaries are not self-defined; if it is not to
be too broadly or self-servingly construed, the circumstances under
which the implied mandate can be said to apply must be specified
and justified. This can be done in two ways. To begin with, one can
try to identify the sorts of issues around which a national consensus
probably exists on the matter of necessary deception—a consensus
revealed in an explicit literature or by the fact that public, legislative,
or scholarly complaints about such subterfuge are rarely, if ever,
voiced, despite evidence of its existence. Further, if consent for deception in the general category has indeed been granted, government
should not shrink from disclosing the fact of the deception if and
when the continued need for it can no longer be reasonably justified.
Consequently, its readiness to do so is a second test of implied consent.

Both methods suggested by our rule may provide democratic justification for the deception of Americans, and we will begin with the
first of the two, by identifying the types of information around which
a national consensus on the need for concealment can be assumed
to exist.

To begin with, Americans are not a priori opposed to every form
of domestically directed deception, but the sentiment is highly qualified. Most important, the public does not condone outright prevar-

ication. Asked whether the president or the government could be justified in lying to the public, substantial majorities regularly reject the notion (table 5.1). The public's tolerance for untruth is no greater when the matter is narrowed to the area of foreign policy (table 5.2). At the same time, there appears to be a greater willingness to accept the need for *secrecy*—since most Americans seem willing to endorse an occasional reliance on secret operations for foreign policy purposes (table 5.3). But this too is qualified for, although it does not seem to believe that general disclosure is always a good idea, the public is reluctant to have information on secret operations kept even from the congressional leadership (table 5.4).

Are there any sorts of political information that are preferentially covered by an assumption of legitimate secrecy? In the opinion of many political commentators and scholars considerable implied consent can be assumed for the need to keep sensitive national defense

---

TABLE 5.1
Lying to the American Public

(A)

"Do you think it is frequently, occasionally, or never alright for the President to lie to the American public?"

Frequently	Occasionally	Never
5%	21%	72%

(B)

"Do you think there are times when the United States government is justified in lying to the American public?"

Sometimes	Never	Not sure
30%	63%	5%

SOURCES: Roper Organization, February 6, 1987 (A). *Los Angeles Times*, December 6, 1986 (B).

TABLE 5.2
Lying for Foreign Policy Purposes

"Suppose the Administration in Washington thinks it must lie to the American people in order to achieve a foreign policy goal. Under those circumstances, is it all right for the Administration to lie to the American people, or isn't it?"

All right	Not all right	Depends
18%	72%	7%

SOURCE: CBS News/*New York Times*, October 24, 1986.

TABLE 5.3
The Acceptability of Secret Operations

(A)
"In your view, secret operations in government are . . ."

Sometimes necessary but only in special circumstances	Often necessary to achieve important objectives	Never justified in our system of government.
58%	27%	15%

(B)
"In his testimony (to the Iran-Contra investigating committee) today, Colonel (Oliver) North said he believes the U.S. government is sometimes justified in conducting secret foreign policy operations in order to protect the national security and further U.S. interests abroad. Do you agree or disagree with North?"

Agree	Disagree
68%	30%

sources: Time/Yankelovich Clancy Shulman, July 9, 1987 (A). ABC News, July 7, 1987 (B).

TABLE 5.4
Secrets from Congress

(A)
"Should a President be allowed to conduct secret operations in foreign countries without notifying the top Congressional leaders of both parties if he thinks it's necessary to do that?"

Yes	No
34%	61%

(B)
"Do you think it was right or wrong for the Reagan Administration to conceal its secret operations in Iran and Nicaragua from Congress?"

Right	Wrong
28%	62%

sources: CBS News/New York Times, July 16, 1987 (A). Yankelovich, Clancy Shulman, July 9, 1987 (B).

information hidden from hostile foreigners—whether through secrecy or more active forms of subterfuge. There is virtually no dissent on this, even from the most vocal advocates of governmental candor. By the same criteria, it is also likely that most people would recognize the need to protect diplomatic negotiations—and even governmental deliberation—from the paralyzing effects of premature disclosure. But it is much less probable that Americans would agree to be deceived about matters of major import with the argument that they could not be trusted to behave in a manner consistent with the national interest. Nor could it credibly be proposed that the nation would agree to be misled about the substance of its government's actual or intended policies. Certainly no empirical evidence or scholarly consensus suggests otherwise.

Avaliable data on public opinion support the gradations of implied consent suggested above. For example, when asked whether the government should be allowed to withhold certain types of information from the press, the public concurred if national security, and to a lesser extent limited military matters, are at issue. At the same time it was much less willing to support secrecy when it was a matter of governmental convenience or its desire to avoid embarrassment (table 5.5, figure 5.1).

Still, the former preferences of the governed are not always apparent, even for the more general rules of governmental behavior, and revealed sentiment is but one of two methods for establishing the existence of implied consent. The second, and occasionally the more useful, rule for establishing its presence is the following: that, as soon as possible, the fact of domestic deception is acknowledged and its justification submitted for democratic approval. If at such time the nation's reaction is clearly supportive, the test of implied consent will have been passed. If the deception is not willingly revealed after the need for it is no longer there, or if it does not meet with domestic approbation when disclosed, there is no reason to assume that there ever was consent. Such justification is most necessary where deception is guided by fear that public pressure would force the wrong policies upon the government (rather than by a need to protect the confidentiality of the government's deliberations or its options during a very exceptional crisis), for in that case the assumption of societal acquiescence is weakest.

TABLE 5.5
Secrecy and the Press

"Do you think the press should publish top secret government material once it comes into their hands, or should it be withheld until the government decides publication will not harm national security?"

Should publish	Should be withheld
14%	76%

SOURCE: Opinion Research Corporation, June 21, 1971.

FIGURE 5.1
Justifications for Keeping Information from the Press
(when secrecy should "always" be maintained)

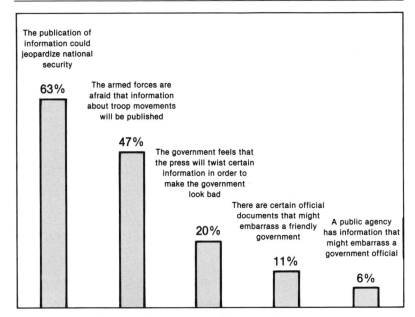

SOURCE: Survey by the *Los Angeles Times*, November 11–17, 1983

In this regard it is important that many cases of revealed deception have not satisfied either of the two criteria for implied democratic consent. To begin with, many instances did not cover the *areas* of policy for which some a priori acceptance of the need for deception could be assumed. Many of the instances that came to public attention during recent decades did not involve a commonly accepted notion of national security—a need to act cautiously under conditions of acute crisis, or to protect the confidentiality of government deliberations or diplomatic negotiations. Second, very rarely was the fact of deception willingly acknowledged and subjected to the test of post hoc democratic endorsement.

One implication is that any attempt to account for secrecy and prevarication must reach beyond the dictates of political realism or the government's wish to discharge a public mandate—beyond the need to deceive hostile foreigners or to keep information from Americans in their own best interest. Even if we do not undertake an empirical examination of the causes of domestically directed governmental deception (an undertaking that is, by its very nature, impracticable), it will be useful at least to suggest some reasons for deception other than those generally invoked on its behalf.

Habitual Sources of Deception

A significant portion of existing secrecy and prevarication may be rooted in the structure of internal governmental interests, i.e., in a logic no broader than that of the machinery of government. Specifically, it may be that deception often stems from one or more of the following three circumstances: (1) competition and rivalry between different segments of the foreign policy bureaucracy, (2) a desire to foreclose dissent within the councils of government, and (3) an attempt to reduce the risk of political embarrassment to the government or to certain of its components, which would be produced by disclosure of its activities.

Bureaucratic Rivalry

It is generally appreciated that the bureaucratic endeavor largely revolves around the desire, in Max Weber's words, "to increase the superiority of the professionally informed by keeping their knowledge and intentions secret."[44] Weber recognized that secrecy, even if initially desired to facilitate pursuit of organizational objectives, often acquires the purpose of insulating the bureaucracy from external control and helping it maintain an edge over competing administrative units. According to Weber, this not only defines bureaucracy's attitude toward the society outside it but also characterizes the stance of its various units and subunits toward one another, because a *principal* motivating drive of individual bureaucracies is to increase their power and position vis—vis other governmental agencies and organizations.[45] I.M. Destler, one of the most thorough students of U.S. foreign policy decision making, observed that the occasionally genuine need for secrecy is "combined with its even more frequent use by officials to increase their influence."[46] To the extent that interbureaucratic power depends substantially on the control of relevant information, the secrecy of these institutions is only incidentally related to motives that realpolitik, or most other conceptions of legitimate policy aims, would endorse.

Within the foreign affairs bureaucracy, for example, the rivalry between the State Department and the staff of the National Security Council has been a defining feature of foreign policymaking during recent history, and the frequent unwillingness of either to share information with the other has reflected their mutual suspicion. The National Security Council and the Pentagon are frequently linked in a similar rivalry. When, for example, Henry Kissinger headed the NSC staff, he appears to have excluded the Joint Chiefs of Staff from information to which they felt entitled. In reponse, they reportedly infiltrated a spy as a clerk at the NSC in order to obtain the information that had been denied them.[47] Early in 1986 Defense Secretary Caspar Weinberger found out that the National Security Agency, the arm of the Pentagon with particular responsibility for electronic intelligence, had, on instructions from the NSC staff, withheld intelligence from him on Iran.[48] Examples of expressly withheld information between bureaucratic units are not hard to come by, and this form of dissembling is more tightly linked to interbureaucratic rivalry than to loftier claims of national policy.

Thwarting Dissent Within Government

At other times, specific policy objectives and the concern that other governmental units would oppose a preferred course of action may account for the deception. The purpose of shutting out intragovernmental dissent was, to all appearances, the reason why those within the NSC staff and the CIA who were privy to the Iran-Contra project kept their plans from the State Department and the Department of Defense, both of which, they anticipated, would object to what they were doing.[49] Similarly, President Reagan's intention of calling, on March 23, 1983, for a massive effort to develop a space-based antimissile defense system was not shared with top officials at the CIA, the State Department, or even the Pentagon. The State Department might, it seems, have objected because of the repercussions for America's NATO allies, and many at the Defense Department were unconvinced of its feasibility.[50] Thus policies associated with particular organizational objectives, and pursued within various recesses of bureaucracy, may be designed to avoid, initially at least, a more general governmental scrutiny that they may not survive.

Avoiding Domestic Political Embarassement

Though deception is sometimes meant to foreclose opposition from other governmental actors, it is also often intended to insulate the government from resistance to its policies from within the broader societal setting to which it is theoretically accountable. The initial prevarication surrounding the U-2 incident was not seriously intended to mislead the Soviets as much as Americans. The same was true of President Nixon's secret bombings of Cambodia in 1969 and 1970. The Reagan administration's misrepresentation of the facts connected with the Iran-Contra affair was, by just about any credible interpretation, primarily designed to avoid domestic political embarrassment. A similar conclusion applies to the secrecy with which President Bush undertook overtures to China in the wake of the violent 1989 crackdown on pro-democracy forces in Beijing. President Johnson's misleading statements in 1964 on his intentions vis—vis the Vietnam War were, it appears, intended to spare him the electoral costs of candor about his own projected policies.

Insulating policymakers from the judgment of the public and Congress when actual policy collides with official pronouncements or with the nation's expressed preferences or tacit values seems to have been the basis for much of the deception that has come to light in recent decades. When, as is most often the case, the deception continues after the act of policy, it cannot be considered primarily an attempt to ensure that the government be permitted to do what it deems best. Its frequent purpose is simply to avoid political accountability for acts that a democratic consensus would punish. It may be ironic that Congressman Richard Nixon complained, on the occasion of the administration's refusal to divulge certain documents related to the MacArthur controversy in 1951, that "the new test for classifying secret documents now seems to be not whether the publication of a document would affect the security of the nation but whether or not it would affect the political security of the Administration."[51]

A similar statement could no doubt be made about other instances of deception.

The closer one examines the purposes of deception, the less one is disposed to assume that it is primarily rooted in the claims of realpolitik or even, more generally, in the requisites of successful policy. That there are occasional benefits to governmental concealment cannot be doubted, and the areas in which there seems to be significant implied consent are those where the benefits are least disputable. But, if much of what is hidden from democratic scrutiny is connected to the internal interests of the various components of government, it is more difficult to argue that, in the aggregate, the benefits overshadow the costs. A survey of the consequences that deception can cause helps place its ledger in more comprehensive perspective.

Some Foreign Policy Consequences

To some extent the sorts of consequences created by government concealment depend on the reasons behind the deception, and they should be discussed in that light. Of the three hypothesized purposes examined in the previous section, the first two involve *intragovernmental* dissembling—either as a means of jockeying for power among bureaucracies or because one unit of government seeks to shut out anticipated dissent from other units. In both cases the inevitable consequence is to restrict information to some of those who have a legitimate stake in the policy. The likelihood that this dominant unit's judgment would be questioned or its authority challenged decreases correspondingly as decisional power is concentrated in a restricted number of policymakers. Apart from the consequences for political pluralism and accountability, this may affect the quality of the resultant policy. The range of perspectives represented is narrowed, the number of options examined is reduced, and all the implications of a given course of action may not be considered. As one administration official explained to the *New York Times* regarding the Iran-Contra affair:

> The checks and balances broke down. You had an NSC group trying to conduct covert operations and going around the main departments, which should have been involved. People who would have known the pitfalls would have said: "This doesn't make sense. It's

going to leak out in Iran," as it did, "because of factional fights there. It's going to damage us among the Saudis." But the people who would have said those things weren't involved.[52]

A special type of risk arises when normative goals, national values, and hypotheses about how the world works are at issue and when the policies of the executive are at odds with the views of those to whom it is politically accountable. Since it is not apparent that the executive's awareness at the normative and contextual level is much better than that of other segments of society, the quality of a foreign policy shrouded in deception is not likely to be appreciably preferable to one conducted in full public view. A further, and generally ignored, consequence of intragovernmental restrictions on effective participation in decision making concerns the specific bent that policy can take—particularly the more extreme character it may assume as a result of the narrowness of the decision-making group. A recent and rigorously designed empirical study compared the type of policies pursued when decision-making authority was exercised (1) by a single individual, (2) by a single homogeneous group, and (3) by a decisional unit comprised of multiple and relatively autonomous groups. The authors concluded that a more extreme variety of foreign policy behavior was produced in the first two instances than was produced by the more moderately disposed system of multiple autonomous groups.[53]

The reasons are not particularly mysterious. The more restricted the number of participants, the fewer the perspectives examined and nuances considered and the easier it is to conceive of either/or, all-or-nothing policies. Rigidity—rather than the adaptability to changing circumstances preferred by political realists as well as many of their critics—may intrude too often into policy, providing one of the internal contradictions of realpolitik. A number of instances of U.S. policy conducted under a thick shroud of secrecy may lend credence to these findings.

The long-term consequences for policy effectiveness may be most substantial when the deception is recognized or suspected. Since some grant of societal support is necessary for the effective conduct of foreign affairs (a matter recognized by advocates of political realism),[54] the erosion of trust in political leaders removes a crucial political resource of democratic government and stands to undermine the foundation for effective policy.

A major cost of uncovered deception is the "credibility gap" it produces—a burden several recent U.S. administrations, most apparently those of presidents Johnson and Nixon, have had to deal with. Berating John Poindexter for the subterfuge he and his National Security Council staff had practiced on Congress in the Iran-Contra affair, Representative Dick Cheney explained that "the reason for not deceiving Congress is a very practical one—it's stupid! It's self-defeating, because while it may in fact allow you to prevail in the problem of the moment, eventually you destroy the president's credibility."[55]

Beyond the president's impaired ability to conduct an effective foreign policy following the revelations of prevarication, the shackles that Congress, generally with public support, is apt to impose on the deceiving executive may hobble his power to conduct policy more than the constraints that greater candor might have entailed. This happened to President Reagan as new legislation was enacted to limit presidential ability to conduct covert operations without congressional knowledge. It also befell Richard Nixon following the revelation of his own deceptive practices, and his waning popularity paralleled the declining belief in his truthfulness. Similarly, Lyndon Johnson's leading biographer, discussing the collapse of his presidency by 1968, observed that "the issue was not simply Johnson's popularity; it was his loss of credibility."[56] If a principal reason for deception is to ensure adequate governmental autonomy, the possibility of counterproductive consequences must be acknowledged.

The Ledger on Deception

Two principal questions were addressed in this chapter: first, whether a sound foreign policy requires that various of its facets at times be concealed from the American public; second, if this is the case, whether this requirement can be compatible with democratic norms. The answer to the second question is a highly qualified affirmative—democratic principle can be preserved as long as there is prior assent of the governed to be misled in that general class of circumstances. In actual fact, indications of such consent are rarely apparent.

The answer to the first question is more complex, but it does not buttress the case for deception associated with realpolitik. Apart from a need to mislead hostile foreigners—an often genuine need whose boundaries are, nevertheless, too fluid and ill defined to provide a satisfactory guide to government behavior—the main justification is related to the theme of disruption from below. One suspects, however, that the case is overstated, for the areas where domestic disclosure stands to impair foreign policy (acute crises, diplomatic negotiations, and intragovernmental deliberations) are few, and most instances of deception are justified by entirely different concerns. In any case, the reason for deception is often at variance with its rationale, which may be more closely connected to the internal purposes of government machinery than to plausible concerns with the quality of policy. Under the circumstances, exaggerated assessments of the dangers of being candid with the nation are coupled with an underestimate of the problem of derailment from above.

Chapter 6

IN SEARCH OF
THE NATIONAL INTEREST

"When I choose a word," Humpty Dumpty said,
in a rather scornful tone, "It means just what
I choose it to mean—neither more nor less."
"The question is," said Alice, "whether you
can make words mean so many things."
"The question is," said Humpty Dumpty,
"which is to be master—that is all."
                       —Lewis Carroll

Our point of departure was the claim, most forcefully made by real-politik, that democratic foreign policy suffers from having to accommodate the sentiments of the public and its representatives, sentiments that are grounded in a combination of factual ignorance and emotive drives that clash with the tenets by which international affairs are best managed. Although political leaders are likely to grasp these principles and wish to conduct foreign relations accordingly, disruption from below prevents them from doing so. The inference is that in a world marked by ruthless competition for power friction between democracy and foreign policy should generally be resolved in favor of the latter. The executive branch of government should be granted more authority than would be proper in the realm of domestic policy. Also, some departure from democratic norms—as reflected in a measure of domestically directed subterfuge—may be unavoidable, and consequently acceptable.

A Two-Dimensional Issue

This thesis has two logically distinct facets. On the one hand, it makes certain assumptions about the *behavioral predispositions* of various segments of the democratic polity (the public, legislators, and professional diplomats) and about the foreign policy implications of these predispositions. On the other hand, and on the basis of its view of the national interest, it posits *criteria* for a sound foreign policy (generally bearing on the dispassionate and prudential management of power) against which the consequences of these behavioral propensities can be assessed. This is a crucial distinction, for it encompasses the ways of addressing misgivings about democratic foreign policy. Although this book finds fault with certain strands of the realist thesis, my conclusions cannot be summarized by its simple rejection. Several judgments on the thesis could be drawn, and in each case a separate reference to each of its two dimensions (the behavioral assumptions and the measures of a good foreign policy) would be necessary.

The Behavioral Assumptions

If one were to adopt the realist conception of a sound foreign policy, as summarized in the three criteria presented in chapter 1, one of two simple conclusions could theoretically have been reached. We could have accepted the behavioral assumptions of realpolitik, agreed that the public and its representatives are not likely to behave as one would wish them to, and concluded that democratic foreign policy is unlikely to be wise or effective. Under the circumstances, a bifurcated conception of democracy, with a less participatory version applying to foreign than to domestic affairs, might be recommended. Or else, we could have rejected the behavioral propositions, and thus realists' concerns about the quality of foreign policy, and urged the full application of democratic principles to the conduct of external relations. But the argument presented thus far does not support such simple conclusions.

Realpolitik is indeed mistaken in what it assumes about the foreign policy predilections of various segments of the American polity. The complication is that it is wrong on *two* levels: not only with regard to the public and its representatives, about whom realists have the most serious misgivings, but about the policy professionals in whom they place their confidence. The public mind reflects rather well the foreign policy principles advocated by political realism. While Congress is more prone to press for the promotion of ideological values abroad, it is not guided by the uninformed demagoguery that is often attributed to it. In short, disruption from below should not be a significant problem. At the same time, while the foreign policy bureaucracy is deeply steeped in the pursuit of its organizational interests, the pressures of democratic political competition promote a pattern of incentives among those whose careers depend on the outcome of presidential elections, often delinking the conduct of foreign affairs from the international circumstances it is supposed to address. Accordingly, derailment from above, especially that associated with electoral competition, may be the greater of the two problems.

Thus, while certain features of democracy may not be compatible with a successful foreign policy, these are not the ones usually mentioned by the followers (witting or unwitting) of classical realists. By the same token, a remedy implied by realist assumptions (increasing foreign policy autonomy at the pinnacle of the political system) is not the solution to which we are led.

The Notion of A Good Foreign Policy

Beyond the matter of the respective competence of government and governed, conclusions are further complicated by the fact that the realist measures of a good foreign policy need not be accepted. This is a very consequential line of thought and, while my central task has been to evaluate the behavioral inclinations of various segments of the U.S. polity, I did not depart very far from the standards of sound policy that realists themselves would endorse. Although this has helped make the discussion both consistent and manageable, the standards of political realism need not be accepted. Accordingly, this chapter represents a sort of extended addendum to the book. It addresses the criteria that are used to evaluate whether foreign policy is wise and successful, criteria that ultimately revolve around some conception of the national interest. The exercise is necessary because no conclusions regarding the impact of democracy on the conduct of international affairs can be truly useful unless it is decided what, ideally, this conduct should aim for. In turn, some justification, in terms of a higher purpose, should be provided. If no such objective purpose can compellingly be argued the implications for our concerns should be carefully considered.

Much criticism of the realist position has come from those who would reach beyond its hard-nosed, and to some minds cynical, conception of desirable foreign policy objectives to include the pursuit abroad of values around which American society is shaped. Occasionally, the argument reflects a conviction that external affairs, especially for a nation capable of making a difference, should aim to make the world a better place in ways not directly measurable by formulas of power acquisition and management.[1] Criticism is also rooted in the belief that, as a practical matter, principles and pragmatism cannot be entirely separated—since a world whose values more closely reflect those of the United States is more likely to be sympathetic to its interests.[2] Moreover, an original line of thinking argues that interest-based policies are fundamentally conservative and static, concerned with the short term and the world as it is, and thus insufficiently adaptive to changing international circumstances. Value-based policies, on the other hand, are more innovative and capable of addressing a world wherein changes are themselves a consequence of shifts in values.[3]

Moreover, the possibility of going beyond the foreign policy aims of traditional realism is not limited to the promotion of political ideals. As an illustration, a variety of economic interests may be worth pursuing internationally even though their bearing on national power is ambiguous. For example, national prosperity, or the increased prosperity of certain segments of society, may be deemed beneficial to the national interest (because of the societal good it implies) even if clearly *detrimental* to power (e.g., because it encourages consumption at the expense of investment or because it involves economic cooperation with rivals).

A conceptual challenge presents itself as we expand the catalogue of legitimate policy objectives beyond those suggested by political realism. If the singleminded pursuit of power-related goals is even partially incompatible with other external objectives, some standard is needed to determine which of the two pursuits is preferable. In turn, this calls for some justification in terms of an independent, and empirically meaningful, measure of a good foreign policy. The only standard general enough to guide the conduct of external affairs is that of the *national interest*, and any discussion of what makes a good foreign policy must rest on this standard.

Defining the National Interest

At least three conditions are generally assumed for *any* interest to qualify as "national." To begin with, it must be sufficiently vital to rank near the top of the society's hierarchy of values. Second, it must be affected by the international environment (a property that distinguishes it from the "public" interest). Finally, it must transcend the affairs of particular individuals and groups to encompass the concerns of the national community. "We are talking," explained one author, "about the interests of the nation state in its entirety, not the interests of private groups, bureaucratic entities, or political organizations within the state."[4] As another observed, the concept "is understood to mean a state of affairs valued solely for its benefit to the nation."[5]

Given these three conditions, what, specifically, does the national interest consist of, and how might it be recognized in practice? Those who have sought an answer have done so in one of two ways. Some have built its substance around a single abstract principle, presumed to embody the three aforementioned conditions. I will call this the *assumptive* strategy. Others have simply identified a list of foreign policy objectives that, by dint of their importance and general societal relevance are deemed proper subsets of the national interest. I will designate this the *enumerative* method.

The Assumptive Approach

It is not surprising that many of the efforts to formulate a conception of the national interest have been produced by realists; and since it is mainly their criteria of desirable foreign policy that we have relied upon in this book, we should address the higher principles, assumed to reflect the national interest, in which these criteria are rooted. From the perspective of realpolitik, the foundation on which a useful conception of the national interest must stand is that of *power*, a conviction that Morgenthau has expressed most vigorously. Explaining that the "main signpost that helps political realism to find its way through the landscape of international politics is the concept of interest defined in terms of power,"[6] he reaches a point of theoretical circularity early in the development of this reasoning. In his opinion, the lust for power stems from an ineradicable urge that is basic to the nature of social life, it is in fact one of those "elemental bio-social drives by which in turn society is created."[7] If some nations are power seekers, it follows that, in an anarchic world, others must be so as well. "The aspiration for power being the distinguishing element of international politics, international politics is of necessity power politics."[8]

But if power is presented both as an end in *itself* and a means toward *other* ends, national interest is not given much analytical substance. Defining power as an end in itself, i.e., identifying its pursuit and management with the national interest, leads to little more than limp tautologies, as many critics have been quick to point out. One is on firmer ground when viewing power as a means to other ends, *security* being the end that is most credibly compatible with power.[9] But this raises a host of problems. As we have already discussed (chapter 5), it is hard to endow the concept of national security with a generally accepted meaning. Even if this were possible, a conception of the national interest reduced to its security component would be considered too narrow. Indeed, most would agree that preserving the integrity of the nation's normative order, promoting the international competitiveness of its economy, and preserving the health of its natural environment, are also vital interests that are but incidentally promoted (and occasionally even undermined) through the pursuit of national power.

In any case, a number of authors loosely associated with political realism have questioned the value of making security and power the defining features of national purpose. Raymond Aron has criticized the inability to distinguish power as end from power as means, pointing out that power "is not in itself a rational objective."[10] At the same time, he has expanded the inventory of national goals far beyond the sole concern with security. Similarly, Arnold Wolfers has shown little sympathy for the tendency to equate security with power,[11] considering that the former has folds of implication not encompassed by the latter. Thus, several realists come closer to approaching the national interest from an enumerative rather than assumptive perspective.

Other realist conceptions of the national interest are particularly elusive. George Kennan frequently speaks of the prudential management of power as a component of the national interest, stressing the need to keep ends and means in rational balance. But when it comes to identifying logically antecedent goals, to which power is instrumental, Kennan slips his realist moorings, drifting from hard-nosed, security-conscious realpolitik to mistier shores. In one of his most explicit statements on the subject, he ventured that "the fundamental interest of our government in international affairs is . . . to assure that we should be permitted, as a people, to continue our Pilgrim's Progress toward a better America under the most favorable conditions, with a minimum of foreign interference, and also with a minimum of inconvenience or provocation to the interests of other nations."[12]

Astonishingly (given what he has had to say on the subject of democracy), Kennan goes much farther than most other political realists in binding the purposes of foreign policy to the preservation of domestic ideals. The national interest, he argues, "is *not* a detached interest in our international environment pursued for *its own sake*, independent of our aspiration and problems here at home. It does not signify things we would like to see happen in the outside world primarily for the sake of the outside world . . . It is the function of our duty to ourselves in our domestic problems.[13]

Several observations can be made regarding Kennan's attempts to elucidate the national interest. To begin with, whatever contribution he makes is only incidentally linked to his views on power—as such its roots in realpolitik are not apparent. Second, he is vague when it comes to specifying the concept's operational meaning. At the level of generality provided many would agree with his notion of America's purpose. But the nebulously abstract character of his definition makes it almost certain that differences would occur on the particulars of such objectives as "a better America under the most favorable conditions." As important, some of the goals he invokes are at least partially incompatible (pursuing one's best interest with "minimum inconvenience" to other nations); because of this, preferences might clash on their respective priority, and he offers no guidelines as to how they should be resolved. At the level of practical conduct, then,

Kennan's conception of the national interest provides few clues to the most desirable directions of U.S. foreign relations. Where he specifies these directions, the guiding principle seems to be the sensible management of national power. But, since this seems to be a means to an end (why else would it be necessary?) rather than an end in itself, the principle provides little indication of the interests that are most vital to the United States.

A different type of assumptive approach defines the national interest not in terms of objectives involved but in terms of the identity of its bearer. History's most obvious illustration was the tendency to equate the concept with that of the *dynastic interest*. A roughly analogous contemporary example is contained in the work of Stephen Krasner, who, in his effort to give the national interest operational content, conceives of it in terms of whatever the government does.[14] He feels that "it is a fundamental error to identify the goals of the state with some summation of the desires of specific individuals or groups."[15] This, in his view, is particularly inadvisable as many individuals or groups can be made better off only by making others worse off. At the same time, he sees little value in Morgenthau's inclination to equate interest with power since, power being pursued essentially for security purposes, it fails to capture other national aims or, indeed, *any* of the national aims of countries that encounter no meaningful threats to their security. It is much better in Krasner's view to consider the national interest as directly defined by the State's (i.e., government's) objectives, as these are revealed in practical policy. Assuming that the government is the only true instrument of societal interests, these interests can be identified empirically by observing the policies it adopts. Any other perspective must be founded on *assumptions* regarding what is good for the nation—and thus reflect the observer's subjective perspective. He specifies, as a restriction, that government policy must pertain to general national objectives (not those of specific groups or individuals) and be pursued over a sufficiently long period of time, if it is to qualify.[16]

Its singular twist notwithstanding, this approach is not really helpful. Even aside from the difficulty of determining what is a general rather than a parochial objective and of deciding how long it must be pursued to qualify as a national interest, the approach is problematic on theoretical grounds. Unlike most conventional approaches to the topic, Krasner's seems to have a descriptive rather than a normative purpose. It is designed to help us decide what to consider as the national interest for research purposes, not to determine what *ought* to be pursued in its name. If this is the case, then it is of little help in distinguishing a good foreign policy from a bad one. If, on the other hand, a normative content is to be assumed, then Krasner's conception leads to the logically and empirically untenable position that, insofar as it pursues what it deems to be general objectives and does so long enough, a government can never act contrary to the national interest. It is unlikely that this is what Krasner means to say.

With the exception of some conceptions of dubious relevance to the American case (the Marxist perspective, for example), these are the major assumptive approaches to the national interest. On the whole, they do not go far toward providing a standard against which to assess the wisdom of foreign policy. Some of their variants lead to circular reasoning, others are much too general, yet others (e.g., the dictum that power should be prudently exercised) are virtually platitudinous.

The Enumerative Approach

Among the authors who have contributed to this approach are several who, like Arnold Wolfers and Raymond Aron, may be termed "qualified" realists, yet others (Alexander George, for example) cannot easily be assigned to any particular body of scholarly doctrine. Each has attempted to establish a set of discrete objectives spanning the national interest without presenting an overarching principle of politics by which they are jointly covered. The objective that is most frequently mentioned is the nation's security—most narrowly defined in terms of its physical survival (i.e., the integrity of its territory and the safety of its population). Typically, such enumerations include the health of the economy as well. The sanctity of the society's basic normative order, of the political and ethical principles by which it is defined, is also generally included (by realists as well as nonrealists).

There is, thus, a subset of foreign policy goals identified with the national interest that academic opinion endows with a strong presumption of validity. Nevertheless, the enumerative approach encounters problems that highlight the unsatisfactory character of *any* conception of the national interest claiming objective applicability. While no standard inventory of national objectives necessarily exhausts the catalogue of vital and general ends, any attempt to expand the list beyond the three values mentioned above (sometimes even beyond the goal of the nation's physical survival) engenders doubts about the new additions' centrality to the national purpose. Robert Osgood, for example, adds the goals of "prestige" and "national aggrandizement."[17] The former is a nebulous concept whose benefits to the nation are not always easy to identify; it is also one whose exact meaning is hard to circumscribe. For example, it might refer to admiration for a nation's ethical principles or of its tangible achievements. In the latter case, it may lead to envy. Where that is the case, prestige is a two-edged sword. If the case for prestige as a vital interest is not easy to make, it is even more difficult to argue the benefits of national aggrandizement (defined by Osgood as "the increase of national power, wealth, and prestige").[18] Aside from the fact that this category overlaps with others, beyond a certain point, aggrandizement may add more liabilities than assets to the national ledger. This has been true of the Soviet Union (which has labored under the burden of an empire sapping the country's strength and vitality); and, as Paul Kennedy and his followers have argued, a pattern of "overstretch" could be a cause of America's relative demise.[19]

According to Aron, "glory" should rank high among the perennial objectives of most nations,[20] a case that is as hard to argue as the term is difficult to define. Some authors also consider ideological goals a component of national interest,[21] a decision with which any serious realist certainly would take issue.[22] Thus, efforts to establish a comprehensive catalogue of national interests can establish a core, but not the *outer boundary*, of an inventory upon which general agreement could be reached.

One might select only those values whose inclusion virtually everyone would agree upon (for example, physical security, economic prosperity, and integrity of normative order). But this would not resolve the issue, since even for such values, the national interest is unambiguously involved only when they are most starkly and dramatically threatened. Beyond that point, the matter becomes increasingly debatable. This is so for two related reasons. First, because of the diminishing marginal utility associated with increasing possession of most of the things that we value, either as individuals or as a nation. In other words, the further one advances in acquiring something that one values (be it tangible or intangible) or the further one seems to be from losing it altogether, the less the incremental utility attached to each additional level of attainment on that good. As a result, it becomes less and less clear whether the last level of attainment is truly a matter of vital national concern. The national interest probably requires the government to combat foreign protectionism if it faces the prospect of economic depression at home. But the importance of doing so is much less apparent if the consequence of this protectionism is to reduce the growth rate of national income from 4 to 2 percent. Similarly, a nuclear deterrent capable of imposing an unacceptable level of retaliatory damage on a nuclear-armed adversary may be essential to national security. The need for actual nuclear superiority is much more debatable.

George and Keohane address the dilemma in the least unsatisfactory, yet not entirely adequate, manner. They do so by limiting each of the goals comprising, in their view, an "irreducible" national interest to their most vital levels. Thus, national security becomes "physical survival," referring only to the survival of the nation's citizens, not to its territorial integrity. Normative order becomes "liberty," referring to the preservation of a "democratic way of life." Prosperity becomes "economic subsistence," defined as the "people's ability to house, clothe and feed themselves."[23] Although this may be the best approach to the problem of diminishing marginal utility characterizing most national goals, it does not necessarily provide them with acceptable operational meaning. For example, it is likely that "physical survival" is something most people have in mind when contemplating vital national interests. But it is just as clear that "democratic way of life" is a matter of degree: its presence or absence is not a matter of some sharp discontinuity, and the point at which it can be said to have been attained is a matter on which reasonable people can differ. Thus, even if one agreed on the values that could, at *some* level, define the national interest, the point at which they are vital enough to qualify would remain uncertain.

The second reason why it is difficult to agree on how the national interest is involved, as one moves beyond the direst threats to an accepted set of needs, is that the more one acquires of a particular value the more apparent will any incompatibilities often become between it and other values. Although this is not logically inevitable, it is a frequent empirical fact. The more one has of one good relative to others, the less acceptable the gap between the two becomes, in some eyes at least, as their respective marginal utilities are compared. At some point, different groups will come to identify more closely with one or another of the colliding values, making the definition of the national interest increasingly a matter of personal belief and perspective and blurring the distinction between private and societal interests.

As an illustration, if the pursuit of national security involves ever-expanding military outlays, growth in the civilian economy may be stifled by resulting inflationary pressures and high interest rates associated with expansive government spending.[24] As the trade-off between security and prosperity becomes increasingly apparent, those with a professional or ideological commitment to military strength as a foundation of national security will view the choices quite differently from those to whom the health of the civilian economy matters more than the added increment of military preparedness.

For example, business leaders as a group have been found to be somewhat more hawkish than most other segments of society;[25] a tendency that is probably related to a combination of essentially conservative outlook and occasionally direct economic interest in military procurement. Nevertheless, when defense outlays expanded in the early years of the Reagan administration at a rate unprecedented in peacetime, causing the federal deficit and interest rates to balloon correspondingly, many businessmen, even some with a direct stake in defense industry, called for cuts in military spending. In April 1982 a Gallup Poll of senior officers of the nation's largest corporations showed that 83 percent desired a trimming of the Pentagon's budget.[26] In October a meeting of the Business Council (the nation's most elite business organization) saw even the leaders of such major defense contractors as United Technologies calling for reduced defense outlays.[27] Accordingly, where at lower levels of defense spending many business interests coincided with military desires for expanded growth, the two began to collide at higher levels of spending.

If, then, an interest must transcend parochial concerns to qualify as "national," progressively fewer can meet the test as one moves away from the most dramatic threats to core national values and as trade-offs between them become more apparent. The final word on

the subject may never be said, but because it so quickly becomes hard
to distinguish between individual and general interests as trade-offs
between needs become apparent, and because it is difficult to identify
a point at which, by virtue of the importance of the purpose, politics
should stop at the water's edge, efforts to set the contours of an
objective national interest are not usually successful.

In most cases, once any operational definition (assumptive or enumerative) of the concept strays, even a little bit, from the most dramatic threats to core national values, what it encompasses simply
reflects the outcome of domestic political gamesmanship. Charles
Beard may have referred with only slight exaggeration to a more
general phenomenon when he reported, more than half a century
ago, "In studying thousands of actions justified by the appellation
'national interest,' I was tempted to conclude that the conception
was simply a telling formula which politicians and private interests
employed whenever they wished to accomplish any particular design
in the field of foreign policy."[28]

There may have been a time when the national interest, as pursued
through foreign policy, was not very densely entangled with the structure of domestic political relations, but such a time has receded into
the past. Although a growing interdependence of domestic and foreign policy accompanied the process of industrialization,[29] the link
has grown ever tighter during the course of the twentieth century.
As the number of domestic groups making claims on the State increased after both world wars, with extensions of suffrage and the
economic responsibilities vested in the State, the range of external
issues remaining insulated from domestic political bargains and rivalries narrowed. In recent decades the expanding shares of GNP
attributed to foreign trade, the mobility of capital across borders, and
the progressive internationalization of financial and securities mar-
kets has made the satisfaction of domestic welfare interests increasingly contingent on the circumstances of their pursuit in other countries. Predictably, the term *intermestic* has been added to the
vocabulary of political science to designate issues that partake equally
of both foreign and domestic policy.

Under the circumstances, an empirically meaningful and generally
accepted concept of the national interest becomes increasingly elusive. If most of what is viewed as the national interest emerges from
a process of bargaining between a variety of interests associated with

specific sectors of society, there is no reason why the final product should be elevated to the level of a transcendent unity—one that can be grasped only by an elite hovering above parochial disputes. To begin with, as I have argued in chapters 4 and 5, these elites are not independent observers of the process perched on some great Archimedean platform. Rather, like other parts of the political system, they are active participants in the bargaining process. Occupants of bureaucratic roles pursue their organization's interests and visions, while those who participate in electoral contests for political position simultaneously submit to and shape the views of those segments of the polity on whose support their quest for office depends. In turn, this implies that there rarely *is* a general interest above some blend or amalgam of group concerns, making it easy to concur with those who stress the limited analytical utility of the term *national interest*.[30] Raymond Aron is probably correct in stating that "the plurality of concrete objectives and of ultimate objectives forbids a rational definition of 'national interest.' "[31] The extent of this plurality depends on the number of interests included in the process of democratic political bargaining.

Ultimately, much of what is represented as the national interest has the status of what March and Simon designate as *nonoperational* organizational goals.[32] These are objectives (for example, justice or welfare) that do not, by their definition, contain the criteria for determining whether they will be advanced by specific actions, even after the fact. To assess how well one is doing with regard to nonoperational goals, it is first necessary to translate them into *subgoals* that, in turn, contain empirical measures of attainment. Although a general consensus can attach to a nonoperational goal, members of the organization may disagree on the subgoals needed to give them empirical meaning, and decisions on how best to pursue the former are generally the product of a bargaining process pursued according to the rules devised by the organization for this purpose.

Thus, there may well be a nonoperational conception of the national interest that virtually everyone would agree upon, and that political elites can apprehend very clearly; but the only meaningful conception from the perspective of actual policy prescriptions is one that is translated into empirically describable subgoals. Thus, while it might be easy to reach a consensus on the importance of strategic stability, there may be disagreement on whether the Strategic Defense

Initiative does or does not serve this objective. Although few would deny that it serves the U.S. interest to encourage economic development in the Third World, many would disagree on the appropriate strategies for achieving this (for instance, aid or private investment) or on the type of development that should be promoted. At a less specific level, people may differ on how to optimize between the partially incompatible goals of national security and national prosperity, or between national security and the constitutional order (for example, with respect to civil liberties or the balance of power between the executive and the legislative branch of government).

The fundamental point is that, in most cases, the validity of foreign policy goals is principally given by the rules of the political process, not by the special insights of government leaders. Where goals clash, there is seldom an external standard by which their *intrinsic* worth can be compared; rather, resolution must depend on a set of procedural rules. To the extent that we can meaningfully speak of such a thing as the national interest, this can be done only at the concept's very core, where the most crucial values are unambiguously endangered. Although they are rarely thus threatened, the concept is called upon to cover an extremely broad range of foreign policy activity. Consequently, what both casual and scholarly discourse refer to as the national interest rarely has the character required for an independent measure of how wisely policies are selected.

The conclusions to which we are led cannot, therefore, be simple; certainly not as simple as suggested by most of those who have had something to say about democracy and foreign policy. To the extent that we are willing to accept the standards of good policy offered by political realism, we would have to conclude that there is some conflict between the two—but that the terms of the incompatibility are virtually the *opposite* of what this doctrine and ultimately much of current wisdom has come to believe. Accordingly, the practices that these beliefs might lead one to condone—specifically the concentration of very substantial foreign policy power in the hands of the executive branch of government, the presidency in particular, as well as a measure of domestically directed deception—have little justification. Moreover, as this excursus on the national interest suggests, the conclusion does not *require* that my assessment of the behavioral inclinations of relevant political actors be accepted. If one remains convinced that realpolitik's criticism of the public and its representatives is well founded and that some political elite has a superior ability to guide the nation's external affairs, one also assumes that there is an objective criterion for establishing how good a foreign policy is over a broad range of foreign policy behavior (otherwise, we could not assert that the elite stands to do a better job). In other words, we assume that there is an knowable national interest.

But if most of what passes for national interest is the product of domestic political bargains, if policies cannot generally be defined as more or less good in terms of either the ends they pursue or the means by which they do so, the major basis upon which their normative evaluation must rest is their conformity to the rules of political process by which they were produced and which do have independent normative value, i.e., to the rules of *democratic procedure*. Under the circumstances, a major basis for defining a good foreign policy is in terms of its adherence to these rules, implying that apparent incompatibilities between democracy and foreign policy should generally be resolved in favor of the former. To summarize, it is possible to speak of an objective national interest only when crucial interests are most gravely threatened (a rare occurrence); in most other circumstances a national interest emerges only from an authentically democratic aggregation of domestic preferences.[33]

"Principled Pragmatism": The Foreign Policy Alternative

Establishing the conduct of external relations on foundations similar to those undergirding domestic policy implies several things. It means that the congressional voice should be heard on matters of general national import in the realm of foreign as well as domestic affairs. It means viewing the public as the repository of presumptively valid interests and opinions on foreign policy, not merely as an object to be molded by executive authority in accordance with the latter's vision of national needs and of political expediency. It requires governmental candor on issues for which there is no demonstrable prior public consent to deception. It involves accepting that the public and legislature should help to determine which international objectives are worth pursuing and the appropriate trade-offs between goals that are wholly or partially incompatible—as well as acccepting that they should participate in balancing ends with costs.

Accordingly, democratic foreign policy implies tethering foreign policy as closely as possible to the preferences, self-expressed or elicited, of the national community whose interests it is meant to serve. The main virtue of a foreign policy thus conceived rests on its relation to the national interest, but its substance might have several distinct features.

It would almost certainly display some *combination* of ethical concerns, parochial interests, and commitment to national power and security, but with no single class of concerns dominating the agenda. This might be termed a policy of *principled pragmatism;* it would be more eclectic than pure realism or authentic idealism but it might be preferable in several ways.

It stands not to be particularly moralistic or ideological, for such are not the pragmatic impulses by which U.S. society is normally driven. In fact, the intensely ideological coloration of much of America's postwar diplomacy has been imparted to it, one suspects, by a leadership bent on mobilizing, by appeal to ethical principle, support for policies desired on geopolitical grounds. By contrast, a foreign policy rooted in societal interests is not likely to exhibit much concern with closed philosophical systems or "ultimate" truth. Consequently, principled pragmatism should be particularly conducive to a pluralistic international order. At the same time, such a policy would not be indifferent to values that lie at the heart of U.S. political culture— especially respect for human rights and liberties. It has been amply demonstrated that, their pragmatism and material concerns notwithstanding, Americans find it hard to operate without a moral compass. But in the absence of sharp ideological prisms, promotion of these values abroad is likely to be addressed directly, rather than determined by the nominal political label of foreign regimes. For example, a democratically-rooted foreign policy would probably have condemned human rights violation by right-wing as well as leftist regimes more evenhandedly than has typically been the case.

Some of the virtues of a democratic foreign policy may be unexpected in light of conventional wisdom. In the view of political realism, it is apt to be too volatile, lurching from extreme to extreme. In fact, the opposite judgment is more appropriate. Lacking firm societal roots, a policy independently conceived by executive authority must often be rationalized by oversimplifying the challenges and exaggerating the stakes. Under the circumstances, the policy's stability is at the mercy of shifting interpretations of the evidence and the political fortunes of decision-makers. Anchored in society's interests and beliefs, which rarely change in an abrupt and discontinuous manner, principled pragmatism should be more stable and coherent. In addition, since democratic pluralism tends to create mutually compensating interests and beliefs, its foreign policies might be less monistic and extreme than those produced at the pinnacle of political authority: particularly given the modes of conduct characteristic of American society, where bargaining, negotiation, and flexible adjustment to evolving conditions are the prevailing ways of addressing competing interests and beliefs. On the whole, then, principled pragmatism may encourage a world closer to the vision of William James and John Dewey than of Machiavelli and Morgenthau.

Misgivings may persist. A foreign policy that reflected the play of democratic forces would remain vulnerable to derailment from above, especially to ensnarement with the political interests of contenders for national office. Nevertheless, the policy's firmer societal roots ought to make it less susceptible to self-serving electoral manipulation. If policy is harnessed to interests and beliefs within the body politic, there should be less occasion to *create* a foreign policy climate tailored to the ambitions of political leaders. Also under the rubric of qualms, government would often fail to achieve foreign policy goals it deemed desirable, for lack of domestic support. This would lead to continued warnings about the costs of democracy. But it is precisely the desirability of goals that fail to garner a democratic consensus that should be questioned.

NOTES

1. The Terms of the Debate

1. Thucydides, *The Peloponnesian War*, 2 vols. (New York: Modern Library, 1951), tr. John Hinsley, Jr., passim.

2. Arthur E. R. Boak and William G. Sinnigen, *A History of Rome to A.D. 565* (New York: Macmillan, 1957), p. 64.

3. Ibid., pp. 76–78.

4. This is discussed, inter alia, in Arthur S. Link, *Wilson the Diplomatist* (Baltimore: Johns Hopkins University Press, 1957), chapters 4 and 5.

5. Quoted in Harry F. Graff, "How Johnson Makes Foreign Policy," *New York Times*, July 4, 1965.

6. One exception is the substantial research on the link between regime type and war-proneness. See especially Bruce M. Russett, *Controlling the Sword: The Democratic Governance of National Security* (Cambridge: Harvard University Press, 1990), chapter 5, and Zeev Maoz and Nasrin Abdolali, "Regime Type and International Violence, 1816–1976,"*Journal of Conflict Resolution* (1989), 29(1): 3–35.

7. John Locke, *An Essay Concerning the True Origins, Extent, and End of Civil Government* [1690] (New York: Harper, 1947): pp. 195–196.

8. Quoted in Carl J. Friedrich, *Foreign Policy in the Making* (New York: Norton, 1938), p. 47.

9. Alexis de Tocqueville, *Democracy in America*, 2 vols. (New York: Knopf, 1945), 1:234–235.

10. Paul Kennedy, *The Rise and Fall of the Great Powers* (New York: Random House, 1987), p. 529.

11. Joseph Nye, *Bound to Lead: The Changing Nature of American Power* (New York: Basic Books, 1990), pp. 219–230.

12. Particularly in the funeral oration of Pericles, Thucydides, *The Peloponnesian War*, 3:245.

13. Niccolò Machiavelli, *The Prince* [1537] (New York: New American Library, 1952), especially chapters 1, 3, 5, 18.

14. Leopold Ranke, *The Theory and Practice of History*, ed. G. G. Iggers and K. Von Moltke (Indianapolis: Bobbs-Merrill, 1973), and Georg G. Iggers, "The Image of Ranke in American and German Historical Thought," *History and Theory* (1961) 2:17–40.

15. Much of his thinking on realpolitik is contained in Friedrich Meinecke, *Machiavellism: The Doctrine of Raison d'Etat and Its Place in Modern History* (New Haven: Yale University Press, 1957). For an excellent analysis of Meinecke's political thought see Richard W. Sterling, *Ethics in a World of Power: The Political Ideas of Friedrich Meinecke* (Princeton: Princeton University Press, 1958).

16. I am not referring to neorealism, whose major concern is with the structural properties of international systems and their consequences and not with the domestic circumstances of foreign policy.

17. For a good discussion of this diversity see Robert G. Gilpin, "The Richness of the Tradition of Political Realism," in Robert O. Keohane, ed., *Neorealism and Its Critics*, (New York: Columbia University Press, 1986), pp. 301–322.

18. Reference to Morgenthau's *Politics Among Nations* here will be to the sixth edition, ed. Kenneth W. Thompson (New York: Knopf, 1985).

19. Hans J. Morgenthau, *Politics Among Nations*, p. 168.

20. Ibid., pp. 166–168.

21. Ibid., p. 168.

22. Reinhold Niebuhr, *Christianity and Power Politics* [1940] (Hamden, Conn.: Archon Books, 1969), p. 65.

23. Walter Lippmann, *The Public Philosophy* (Boston: Little, Brown, 1955), chapter 2.

24. Ibid., pp. 23–24.

25. Hans J. Morgenthau, *The Purpose of American Politics* (New York: Knopf, 1960), pp. 274–280.

26. George F. Kennan, *The Cloud of Danger: Current Realities of American Foreign Policy* (Boston: Little, Brown, 1977), p. 6.

27. Stanley Hoffmann, "Restraints and Choices in American Foreign Policy," *Daedalus* (Fall 1962), p. 681.

28. Zbigniew Brzezinski and Samuel Huntington, *Political Power: USA-USSR* (New York: Viking, 1968), p. 382.

29. On the foreign policy principles that guided the founding fathers see Felix Gilbert, *To the Farewell Address: Ideas of Early American Foreign Policy* (Princeton: Princeton University Press, 1961).

30. Antoine Nicolas de Condorcet, *Oeuvres*, 12 vols. (Paris: Firmin Didot, 1847–1849), 9:41–46.

31. James Bryce, *Modern Democracies*, 2 vols. (New York: Macmillan, 1921), 2:379.

32. Kennan, *Cloud of Danger*, p. 4.

33. The argument is very insightfully made in Michael J. Smith, *Realist Thought from Weber to Kissinger* (Baton Rouge: Louisiana State University Press, 1986), chapter 2.

34. See especially Guenther Roth and Claus Wittich, eds., *Economy and Society* (Berkeley: University of California Press, 1978), pp. 215–270; see also Smith, *Realist Thought*, chapter 2.

35. Theodore J. Lowi, *The Personal President: Power Invested, Promise Unfulfilled* (Ithaca: Cornell University Press, 1985), chapters 2 and 3.

36. Samuel Kernell, *Going Public: New Strategies of Presidential Leadership* (Washington, D.C.: Congressional Quarterly Press, 1986).

37. For example, Henry A. Kissinger, *A World Restored: Metternich, Castlereagh, and the Problems of Peace, 1812–1822* (Boston: Houghton Mifflin, 1957), pp. 318–320.

38. Kissinger, *A World Restored*, p. 317. See also the discussion of Kissinger in Smith, *Realist Thought*, pp. 199–203.

39. George F. Kennan, *American Diplomacy: 1900–1950* (Chicago: University of Chicago Press, 1950), p. 176.

40. This is discussed in Miroslav Nincic, *United States Foreign Policy: Choices and Tradeoffs* (Washington D.C.: Congressional Quarterly Press, 1988), pp. 121–126.

41. "Making Democracy Safe for the World," in James N. Rosenau, ed., *Domestic Sources of Foreign Policy* (New York: Free Press, 1967), p. 315.

42. Thomas Babington Macaulay, "Your Constitution is All Sail and No Anchor," letter to Henry S. Randall, October 9, 1858, reprinted in Henry Steel Commager, *America in Perspective: The United States Through Foreign Eyes* (New York: Random House, 1947), p. 353.

43. See, for example, Max Beloff, *Foreign Policy and the Democratic Process* (Baltimore: Johns Hopkins University Press, 1955), pp. 66–68.

44. Joseph S. Nye, Jr., *Bound to Lead: The Changing Nature of American Power* (New York: Basic Books, 1990), pp. 220–221.

45. Kenneth W. Waltz, *Foreign Policy and Democratic Politics: The American and British Experience* (Boston: Little, Brown, 1967), p. 308.

46. Examples include Murray Gilbert, *The Ordeal of This Generation* (New York: Harper, 1929), James T. Shotwell, *Intelligence and Politics* (New York: Harcourt Brace, 1921), and Alfred E. Zimmern, *Neutrality and Collective Security* (Chicago: University of Chicago Press, 1936).

47. Joseph A. Schumpeter, *Imperialism and Social Classes* (New York: August M. Kelley, 1955), p. 33.

48. For example, Arthur M. Schlesinger, Jr., *The Imperial Presidency* (Boston: Houghton Mifflin, 1973) and Henry Steel Commager, *The Defeat of America: Presidential Power and the National Character* (New York: Simon & Schuster, 1974).

49. Schlesinger, *The Imperial Presidency*, pp. ix–x.

50. Richard M. Nixon, *RN: The Memoirs of Richard M. Nixon* (New York: Grosset & Dunlap, 1978), p. 763.

51. Interview with Marvin Kalb, June 17, 1971, *Congressional Record* (June 24, 1971), p. 6627.

52. The quotation is from a letter addressed to Jefferson. See S. Padover, ed., *The Complete Madison* (New York: Harper, 1953), p. 258.

53. Edward A. Shils, *The Torment of Secrecy* (Glencoe, Ill.: Free Press, 1956), especially chapters 6 and 9.

54. Specialists in the theory of international relations will readily recognize the principal sources of these propositions. The most relevant works are Hans J. Morgenthau's *Politics Among Nations: Scientific Man vs. Power Politics* (Chicago: University of Chicago Press, 1946), *In Defense of the National Interest* (New York: Knopf, 1951), and "American Diplomacy: The Dangers of Righteousness," *New Republic* (October 11, 1951), pp. 17–20; George Kennan's *Realities of American Foreign Policy* (Princeton: Princeton University Press, 1954), *Russia: The Atom and the West* (London: Oxford University Press, 1958), *American Diplomacy, Cloud of Danger*, and *The Nuclear Delusion: Soviet-American Relations in the Atomic Age* (New York: Pantheon, 1976); Walter Lippmann's *U.S. Foreign Policy: Shield of the Republic* (Boston: Atlantic–Little, Brown, 1943), *The Cold War: A Study in United States Foreign Policy* (New York: Harper Torchbooks, 1972); Henry Kissinger's *A World Restored: Nuclear Weapons and Foreign Policy* (Garden City, N.Y.: Doubleday, 1957), *The Necessity for Choice: Prospects of American Foreign Policy* (New York: Harper, 1960), *American Foreign Policy* (New York: Harper, 1960), *American Foreign Policy: Three Essays* (New York: Norton, 1969); Reinhold Niebuhr's *Christianity and Foreign Policy*, "The Illusion of World Government," *Foreign Affairs* (April 1949), pp. 379–388.

2. The Mentality of the Masses

1. Bernard C. Cohen, *The Public's Impact on Foreign Policy* (Boston: Little, Brown, 1973).

2. Zbigniew Brzezinski, *Power and Principle: Memoirs of the National Security Advisor* (New York: Farrar, Straus & Giroux, 1983), p. 525.

3. Robert Weissberg, *Public Opinion and Popular Government* (Englewood Cliffs, N.J.: Prentice Hall, 1976), pp. 19–20.

4. Alan D. Monroe, "Consistency Between Public Preferences and National Policy Decisions," *American Politics Quarterly* (January 1979), pp. 3–19.

5. Benjamin I. Page and Robert Y. Shapiro, "Effects of Public Opinion on Policy," *American Political Science Review* (1983), 77:182.

6. Bruce M. Russett, "Democracy, Public Opinion, and Nuclear Weapons," in Philip Tetlock et al., eds., *Society and Nuclear War* (New York: Oxford University Press, 1989).

7. Weissberg, *Public Opinion and Popular Government*, p. 33.

8. Poll taken by the Roper Organization, December 6–13, 1975.

9. Adam Clymer, "Perceptions of America's World Role Ten Years After Vietnam," paper presented at the annual meeting of the American Political Science Association, New Orleans, September 1985.

10. *Harris Survey*, November 26, 1984, p. 3.

11. Lloyd A. Free and Hedley Cantril, *The Political Beliefs of Americans* (New York: Simon & Schuster, 1968), p. 60.

12. "Americans Falter on Geography Test," *New York Times*, July 28, 1988.

13. Reported in David W. Moore, "The Public is Uncertain," *Foreign Policy* (Summer 1979), pp. 70–71.

14. Alexis de Tocqueville, *Democracy in America*, 2 vols. (New York: Knopf, 1945), 2:136.

15. See G. Bingham Powell, Jr., *Contemporary Democracies: Participation, Stability, and Violence* (Cambridge: Harvard University Press, 1982), chapter 2.

16. C. M. Bowra, *Classical Greece* (New York: Time, 1965), p. 108.

17. *The Gallup Poll*, various issues.

18. James N. Rosenau, *Public Opinion and Foreign Policy* (New York: Random House, 1961).

19. For example, Johan Galtung, "Foreign Policy Opinion as a Function of Social Position," in James N. Rosenau, ed., *International Politics and Foreign Policy* (New York: Free Press, 1969), pp. 551–572.

20. George H. Gallup, *The Gallup Poll: Public Opinion, 1988*, (Wilmington, Del.: Scholarly Resources, 1989), pp. 249–250.

21. George F. Kennan, *American Diplomacy: 1900–1950* (Chicago: Univeristy of Chicago Press, 1957), p. 93.

22. Arthur Schlesinger, Jr., "The Cold War Revisited," *New York Review of Books*, October 25, 1979, p. 17.

23. Quoted in Center for Defense Information, *The Defense Monitor* (1985), 3(15):2.

24. Rosenau, *Public Opinion and Foreign Policy*, p. 35.

25. Philip Converse, "The Nature of Belief Systems in Mass Publics," in David Apter, ed., *Ideology and Discontent* (New York: Free Press, 1964), pp. 206–261.

26. Galtung, "Foreign Policy Opinion," pp. 554–560.

27. Cited in Richard Hofstadter, *The American Political Tradition* (New York: Vintage, 1973), p. 6.

28. Kennan, *American Diplomacy*, p. 59.

29. Adam Ulam, *Dangerous Relations* (New York: Oxford University Press, 1983), p. 7.

30. George F. Kennan, *The Nuclear Delusion: Soviet-American Relations in the Atomic Age* (New York: Pantheon, 1983), p. 229.

31. See Miroslav Nincic, *Anatomy of Hostility* (San Diego: Harcourt Brace Jovanovich, 1989), chapter 3, and Peter Filene, *Americans and the Soviet Experiment: 1917–1933* (Cambridge: Harvard University Press, 1967), chapter 2.

32. Rita James Simon, *Public Opinion in America: 1936–1970* (Chicago: Markham Books, 1974), p. 135.

33. Ibid., p. 153.

34. George H. Gallup, *The Gallup Poll: Public Opinion, 1935–1971* (New York: Random House, 1972), pp. 583, 682.

35. Ibid., p. 965.

36. Ibid., p. 1227.

37. Samuel Stouffer, *Communism, Conformity, and Civil Liberties* (Garden City, N.Y.: Doubleday, 1955), pp. 43–44.

38. *The Gallup Poll, 1935–1971*, p. 1201.

39. Reinhold Niebuhr, *Christianity and Power Politics* [1940] (Hamden: Archon Books, 1969), p. 68.

40. Gabriel Almond, *The American People and Foreign Policy* (New York: Praeger, 1950), p. 55.

41. John E. Reilly, ed., *American Public Opinion and U.S. Foreign Policy* (Chicago: Chicago Council on Foreign Relations, 1983), p. 15. See also Miroslav Nincic, *United States Foreign Policy: Choices and Tradeoffs* (Washington D.C.: Congressional Quarterly Press, 1988), chapter 4.

42. *Harris Survey*, May 28, 1984, p. 3.

43. William Schneider, "Rambo and Reality: Having It Both Ways," in Kenneth A. Oye, Robert J. Leiber, and Donald Rothchild, eds., *Eagle Resurgent? The Reagan Era in American Foreign Policy* (Boston: Little, Brown, 1987), p. 47.

44. *Gallup Opinion Index*, 1990.

45. "Factors in America's Greatness," *Current Opinion* (January 1976), p. 2.

46. *Gallup Poll* and *Gallup Opinion Index*, various issues.

47. See Russett, *Democracy, Public Opinion*, p. 73.

48. George H. Gallup, *The Gallup Poll: Public Opinion, 1980* (Wilmington, Del.: Scholarly Resources, 1981), p. 52.

49. *Harris Survey*, May 9, 1983.

50. Elsewhere, I have termed this the "politics of opposites." This thesis and the illustrations below are discussed in greater detail in Miroslav Nincic,

"The United States, the Soviet Union, and the Politics of Opposites," *World Politics* (July 1988), pp. 455-476.

51. Sources for the above are given in Nincic, "The United States."

52. Quoted in Walter Lafeber, *Inevitable Revolutions: the United States in Central America* (New York: Norton, 1983), p. 5.

53. *Gallup Report*, July 1984, p. 26.

54. *Harris Survey*, July 13, 1987, p. 1.

55. *Harris Survey*, April 14, 1986, p. 1.

56. *Gallup Poll: Public Opinion, 1935-1971*, p. 1807.

57. *Gallup Opinion Index*, January 1980, p. 3.

58. *Harris Survey*, February 13, 1986, p. 1.

59. *Harris Survey*, May 21, 1989.

60. "The Public Assesses the Reagan Record on Foreign Policy," *Public Opinion* (Summer 1986), p. 30.

61. *Harris Survey*, September 21, 1987, p. 2.

62. *The Gallup Poll, 1935-1971*, p. 1933.

63. Weissberg, *Public Opinion and Popular Government*, p. 235.

64. Ibid., p. 235.

65. Bruce Jentleson, "The Pretty Prudent Public,"*International Studies Quarterly*, forthcoming.

66. V. O. Key, *Public Opinion and American Democracy* (New York: Knopf, 1961), p. 235.

67. James Rosenau, *Citizenship Between Elections* (New York: Free Press, 1974), p. 45.

68. John E. Reilly, "America's State of Mind," *Foreign Policy* (Spring 1987), p. 43.

69. Converse, "The Nature of Belief Systems," pp. 210-245.

70. For example, Pamela J. Conover and Stanley Feldman, "How People Organize the Political World: A Schematic Model," *American Journal of Political Science* (1984), 28:95-126; see also George E. Marcus, Daniel Tabb, and John L. Sullivan, "The Application of Individual Differences Scaling to the Measurement of Political Ideologies," *American Journal of Political Science* (1974), 18:405-420.

71. Notably, Jon Hurwitz and Mark Peffley, "How Are Foreign Policy Attitudes Structured? A Hierarchical Model," *American Political Science Review* (December 1987), 81:1099-1119.

72. William R. Caspary, "The 'Mood Theory': A Study of Public Opinion and Foreign Policy," *American Political Science Review* (1970), 64:536-546.

73. Robert Y. Shapiro and Benjamin I. Page, "Foreign Policy and the Rational Public," *Journal of Conflict Resolution* (June 1988), 32:220-221.

74. Bruce M. Russett, *Controlling the Sword: the Democratic Governance of National Security* (Cambridge: Harvard University Press, 1990), p. 91.

75. Russell Neuman, *The Paradox of Mass Politics: Knowledge and Opinion in the American Electorate* (Cambridge: Harvard University Press, 1986). See also Eric R. A. N. Smith, *The Unchanging American Voter* (Berkeley: University of California Press, 1989), and Robert P. Luskin, "Measuring Political Sophistication," *American Journal of Political Science* (1987), 31:856–899.

76. Elmo Roper, "So the Blind Shall Not Lead," *Fortune* (February 1942), p. 102.

77. For further discussion of the similarities and differences between public and leaders see Eugene R. Wittkopf, *Faces of Internationalism: Public Opinion and American Foreign Policy* (Durham N.C.: Duke University Press, 1990).

78. The best discussion of these questions of which I am aware is Robert Dahl, *Controlling Nuclear Weapons: Democracy Versus Guardianship* (Syracuse: Syracuse University Press, 1985), especially chapters 3 and 4.

79. Charles E. Lindblom and David K. Cohen, *Usable Knowledge: Social Science and Social Problem Solving* (New Haven: Yale University Press, 1962), p. 11.

80. On the use of analogies in foreign policy analysis see Ernest R. May, *'Lessons' of the Past* (New York: Oxford University Press, 1973).

81. David H. Fischer, *Historians Fallacies: Toward a Logic of Historical Thought* (New York: Harper & Row, 1970), p. 259.

82. See Robert Jervis, *Perception and Misperception in International Politics* (Princeton: Princeton University Press, 1976), pp. 271–279, and Zeev Maoz, *National Choices and International Processes* (London: Cambridge University Press, 1989), pp. 118–120.

83. Carl J. Friedrich, *Foreign Policy in the Making* (New York: Norton, 1938), p. 60.

3. The Conduct of Congress

1. J. William Fulbright, "Congress and Foreign Policy," United States Commission on the Organization of the Government for the Conduct of Foreign Policy, *Congress and Executive-Legislative Relations* (June 1975), 5:58.

2. Quoted in "Congress Is Urged to Retake Power," *New York Times*, October 12, 1973.

3. J. William Fulbright, "Congress and Foreign Policy, Appendix L.

4. Richard M. Nixon, *RN: Memoirs of Richard Nixon* (New York: Grosset & Dunlap, 1978), p. 889.

5. Henry A. Kissinger, *Years of Upheaval* (Boston: Little, Brown, 1982), p. 510.

6. Gerald R. Ford, *A Time to Heal: The Autobiography of Gerald Ford* (New York: Harper & Row, 1979), pp. 345–346.

7. Quoted in "Foreign Affairs . . . He Shall Make Treaties," *National Journal* (May 29, 1976), p. 736.

8. *New York Times*, October 19, 1983.

9. See, for example, Cecil V. Crabb, Jr., and Pat M. Holt, *Invitation to Struggle: Congress, the President, and Foreign Policy*, 2d ed. (Washington D.C.: Congressional Quarterly Press, 1984).

10. George F. Kennan, *The Cloud of Danger: Current Realities of American Foreign Policy* (Boston: Little, Brown, 1977), p. 6.

11. For a discussion of this issue see Benjamin I. Page, "Representation As Well As Competence: Congress and President in U.S. Foreign Policy," Working Paper Series, The Nelson Rockfeller Center for the Social Sciences, Dartmouth College, 1987. For claims regarding relative congressional incompetence in important foreign policy matters see L. Gordon Krovitz and Jeremy Rabkin, eds., *The Fettered Presidency: Legal Constraints on the Executive Branch* (Washington D.C.: American Enterprise Institute, 1989), and Gordon S. Jones and John A. Marini, eds., *The Imperial Congress: Crisis in the Separation of Powers* (Washington, D.C.: The Heritage Foundation, 1988).

12. I. M. Destler, "Executive-Congressional Conflict in Foreign Policy," in Lawrence C. Dodd and Bruce I. Oppenheimer, eds., *Congress Reconsidered*, 2d ed. (Washington, D.C.: Congressional Quarterly Press, 1981), pp. 342–363.

13. John Spanier, *The Truman-MacArthur Controversy and the Korean War* (New York: Norton, 1965), p. 226.

14. Graham T. Allison, *The Essence of Decision* (Boston: Little, Brown, 1971), p. 1.

15. Robert F. Kennedy, *Thirteen Days: A Memoir of the Cuban Missile Crisis* (New York: Norton, 1969), pp. 43–54.

16. See, for example, Bruce Jentleson, "American Diplomacy: Around the World and Along Pennsylvania Avenue," in Thomas E. Mann, ed., *A Question of Balance: The President, the Congress and Foreign Policy* (Washington, D.C.: Brookings Institution, 1989), pp. 146–200.

17. Quoted in " 'Info Gap' Plagues Attempts to Grapple with Growing Executive Strength," *National Journal* (March 17, 1973), p. 381.

18. Thomas M. Franck and Edward Weisband, *Foreign Policy by Congress*, (New York: Oxford University Press, 1979), p. 228.

19. "Bush Bid to Fix Beijing Ties Strains Those with Hill," *Congressional Quarterly Weekly Report* (December 16, 1989), p. 3435.

20. Alyson Pyte, "Congress is Using Aid As a Lever to Protest Rights Abuses," *Congressional Quarterly Weekly Report* (May 13, 1989), p. 1134.

21. Walter Lippmann, "The Ideal of Representative Government," in Clinton Rossiter, ed., *The Essential Lippmann: A Political Philosophy for Liberal Democracy* (New York: Random House, 1963) p. 255.

22. Warren E. Miller and Donald E. Stokes, "Constituency Influence in Congress," in Angus Campbell, Philip E. Converse, Warren E. Miller, and

Donald E. Stokes, eds., *Elections and the Political Order* (New York: John Wiley, 1966).

23. Miroslav Nincic and Barbara Hinckley, "Foreign Policy and the Evaluation of Presidential Candidates," *Journal of Conflict Resolution* (June 1991), pp. 333–335.

24. See, for example, Morton H. Halperin, *Bureaucratic Politics and Foreign Policy* (Washington, D.C.: Brookings Institution, 1974), especially chapter 3.

25. This theme is cogently developed in Allison, *The Essence of Decision;* see also Morton H. Halperin and Arnold Kanter, "Leaders vs. Bureaucrats," in Robert J. Art and Robert Jervis, eds., *International Politics: Anarchy, Force, Political Economy, and Decision-Making,* 2d ed. (Boston: Little, Brown, 1985).

26. As one political scientist correctly observed, "Since public bureaucracy is concerned with special and limited aspects of public policy, to a degree it resembles the ordinary pressure group." Leiper J. Freeman, "The Bureaucracy in Pressure Politics," in Francis E. Rourke, ed., *Bureaucratic Power in National Politics* (Boston: Little, Brown, 1965), p. 28.

27. For a critique of the foreign policy consequences of congressional committees see John Spanier and Eric Uslander, *American Foreign Policy: The Democratic Dilemmas,* 4th ed. (New York: Holt, Rinehart and Winston, 1955).

28. Quoted in *Congressional Quarterly Weekly Report* (April 14, 1984), p. 870.

29. See "Leahy's Departure from Panel Followed Leak to a Reporter," *Congressional Quarterly Weekly Report* (August 1, 1987), pp. 1741–1742.

30. Kissinger, *Years of Upheaval,* p. 179.

31. Halperin, *Bureaucratic Politics,* pp. 173–189.

32. Adlai Stevenson, "Discussion," in Benjamin I. Page, "Representation As Well As Competence," p. 36.

33. The Gulf of Tonkin resolution was regarded by President Johnson as the functional equivalent of a declaration of war; however, it was the product of misleading information on the Gulf of Tonkin incident. On January 11, 1991, both the Senate and the House of Representatives passed resolutions authorizing President Bush to use military force to force Iraq out of Kuwait, if it did not itself withdraw by January 15. This followed a sober and sophisticated debate on the merits of alternative courses of action, and it may be considered tantamount to a contingent declaration of war.

34. Through a concurrent resolution the War Powers Act initially allowed Congress to force the withdrawal of U.S. troops engaged overseas. This provision was nullified by the Supreme Court in 1983 when it struck down the legislative veto.

35. Quoted in Louis Fisher, *Constitutional Conflicts Between Congress and the President* (Princeton: Princeton University Press, 1985), p. 293.

36. Franck and Weisband, *Foreign Policy by Congress*, p. 64.
37. Jacob E. Cook, ed., *The Federalist* (Middletown, Conn.: Wesleyan University Press, 1961), p. 166.
38. *Fleming v. Page*, 9 Howard 601 (1850).
39. On this opinion and the steel seizure case more generally see P. G. Kauper, "The Steel Seizure Case," *Michigan Law Review* (December 1952), and Edward S. Corwin, "The Steel Seizure Case: A Judicial Brick Without Straw," *Columbia Law Review* (January 1953).
40. Statement of Arthur S. Schlesinger, Jr., *War Powers*, Hearings of the Subcommittee on National Security Policy and Scientific Development of the Committee on Foreign Affairs, House of Representatives, 93d Cong., 1st sess., March 1973, 2:171.
41. Louis Henkin, "Foreign Affairs and the Constitution," *Foreign Affairs* (Winter 1987–88), 66:290.
42. *Congressional Quarterly Weekly Report* (June 24, 1989), no. 25, p. 1563.
43. The distinction between war and hostilities short of war has a long pedigree. It corresponds to the line drawn by Hugo Grotius in the seventeenth century between "perfect" and "imperfect" wars. See *The Law of War and Peace* [1625] (New York: Bobbs Merrill, 1925). This distinction was again taken up by Jean Jacques Burlamaqui, whose work was widely consulted during the eighteenth century. Burlamaqui explained that "a perfect war is that which intirely [sic] interrupts the tranquility of the state, and lays a foundation for all possible acts of hostility. An imperfect war, on the contrary, is that which does not intirely interrupt the peace, but only in certain particulars, the public tranquility being in other respects undisturbed." *The Principle of Natural and Political Law*, 7th ed. (Dublin: University Press, 1819), p. 258.
44. This, for example, is the view of Eugene Rostow, "Great Cases Make Bad Law: The War Powers Act," *Texas Law Review* (May 1972), 50:833–900. For the opposite view see Charles A. Lofgren, "On War-Making, Original Intent and Ultra-Whiggery," *Valparaiso University Law Review* (Fall 1986), 21:53–68.
45. "Statement of W. Taylor Reveley III," in *War Powers*, 2:238.
46. *American Bar Association Journal* (March 1984).
47. For a further discussion of relevant constitutional interpretations see Michael J. Glennon, *Constitutional Diplomacy* (Princeton: Princeton University Press, 1990), chapter 3.
48. Quoted in Sarah Glazer, "Making Foreign Policy," *Editorial Research Reports* (June 26, 1987), p. 324.
49. For some of the forces that, in the United States, may cause limited military engagements to escalate beyond the expectations of their initiators see Miroslav Nincic, *United States Foreign Policy: Choices and Tradeoffs* (Washington, D.C.: Congressional Quarterly Press, 1988), chapter 10.

50. A particularly difficult decision is how to treat a *show* of force, the intent of which is to produce a psychological effect rather than combat. Even here, there generally is some escalatory potential, yet it would be very difficult to justify congressional control of what is predominantly a diplomatic rather than a military move.

51. Julian P. Boyd, ed., *The Papers of Thomas Jefferson*, 24 vols. (Princeton: Princeton University Press, 1958), 15:397.

52. Quoted in Sarah Glazer, "Making Foreign Policy," p. 322.

53. For instance, see Eugene Rostow, "Once More unto the Breach: The War Powers Resolution Revisited," *Valparaiso University Law Review* (Fall 1986), 18:1–52.

54. Although the judicial branch of government has traditionally shied away from involvement in foreign policy, a noteworthy recent development in its view of war powers was associated with Operation Desert Shield in 1990. In *Ronald V. Dellums et al. v. George Bush* fifty-four Democratic members of Congress sought a court order forbidding the President from undertaking hostilities against Iraq without a congressional declaration of war. The judge, ruling that it would be inappropriate to issue such an injunction unless it was sought by a congressional majority, nevertheless concluded that Article I of the Constitution left no doubt that the framers intended that a president could not go to war in the absence of congressional approval. For a brief description of this ruling see "Lawmakers Lose Powers Suit," *New York Times*, December 14, 1990, p. A15.

55. Contrary to what is often assumed, the Senate does not actually ratify treaties. Rather, it votes a resolution of ratification (which may include amendments and other qualifications brought by the Senate to the negotiated treaty). If the resolution is accepted, it is sent to the president, who then signs an instrument of ratification.

56. There are further subcategories of executive agreements. For a comprehensive survey, see "Treaties and Other International Agreements: The Role of the United States Senate" (Washington, D.C.: Congressional Research Service, 1984).

57. Louis Fisher, *The President and Congress: Power and Policy* (New York: Free Press, 1972).

58. Mary H. Cooper, *Treaty Ratification*, Editorial Research Reports, *Congressional Quarterly* (1988), p. 41.

59. Respectively: 301 US 324 (1937), 274 and, 315 US 203 (1942), 110, 274.

60. *Le Droit des gens ou principes de la loi naturelle appliqués a la conduite et aux affaires des nations et des souverains* [translation of the edition of 1758] (New York: Oceana Publications, 1964), 3:160.

61. Louis Fisher, *The Constitution Between Friends: Congress, the President, and the Law* (New York: St. Martin's, 1978), p. 204.

62. Franck and Weisband, *Foreign Policy by Congress*, p. 141.

63. On this category of executive agreement see John Norton Moore, "Executive Agreements and Congressional Executive Relations," *Treaty Termination: Hearings Before the Committee on Foreign Relations, U.S. Senate* (Washington, D.C., April 9–11, 1979).

64. Loch K. Johnson, *The Making of International Agreements: Congress Confronts the Executive* (New York: New York University Press, 1984), p. 25.

65. Quoted in "Members Seek Veto over Executive Agreements," *Congressional Quarterly Weekly Report* (August 2, 1975), p. 1713.

66. Senator Clifford Case, *Congressional Record* (June 19, 1972), S9641.

67. Leslie H. Gelb, "A Domestic Challenge to Executive Agreements," *New York Times*, August 17, 1975, p. D2.

68. Ibid.

69. See "Treaties and Other International Agreements," Congressional Research Service, pp. 171–177.

4. Electoral Politics and the Water's Edge

1. The following are some general yet basic works in the analysis of presidential elections: Herbert B. Asher, *Presidential Elections and American Politics*, 3d ed. (Homewood, Ill.: Dorsey Press, 1984); Angus Campbell, Phillip E. Converse, Warren E. Miller, and Donald E. Stokes, *The American Voter* (New York: John Wiley, 1960); Robert D. Cantor, *Voting Behavior and Presidential Elections* (Itasca, Ill.: F. E. Peacock, 1975); Morris P. Fiorina, *Retrospective Voting in American Elections* (New Haven: Yale University Press, 1981); Arthur H. Miller and Martin P. Wattenberg, "Throwing the Rascals Out: Policy and Performance Evaluations of Presidential Candidates, 1952–1980," *American Political Science Review (June 1985)*, 79:359–372; Benjamin I. Page, *Choices and Echoes in Presidential Elections: Rational Man and Electoral Democracy* (Chicago: University of Chicago Press, 1978); Nelson W. Polsby and Aaron B. Wildavsky, *Presidential Elections*, 5th ed. (New York: Charles Scribner's, 1983).

2. See David B. Hill and Norman R. Luttberg, *Trends in American Electoral Behavior* (Itasca, Ill.: F. E. Peacock, 1980), chapter 2.

3. For arguments and evidence stressing the importance of images see Miller and Wattenberg, "Throwing the Rascals Out"; Arthur Miller, Martin P. Wattenberg, and Oksana Malanchuk, "Schematic Assessments of Presidential Candidates," *American Political Science Review* (June 1986), 80:521–540; Donald E. Stokes, "Some Dynamic Elements of Contests for the Presidency," *American Political Science Review* (1966), 60:19–28. For an emphasis on the importance of issues, see V. O. Key, *The Responsible Electorate* (New York: Vintage, 1966); see also the analyses of the 1976, 1980, and 1984 elections conducted by Gerald M. Pomper.

4. Miller and Wattenberg, "Throwing the Rascals Out," p. 365.

5. For the influence of foreign policy on the outcome of presidential elections see John Aldrich, John Sullivan, and Eugene Brogatt, "Foreign Affairs and Issue Voting: Do Presidential Candidates 'Waltz' Before a Blind Audience?" *American Political Science Review* (1989), 83(1):123–141; see also Miroslav Nincic and Barbara Hinckley, "Foreign Policy and the Evaluation of Candidates," *Journal of Conflict Resolution* (June 1991).

6. See, for example, Jong R. Lee, "Rallying Around the Flag: Foreign Policy Events and Presidential Popularity," *Presidential Studies Quarterly* (Fall 1977), 7:252–256; Charles W. Ostrom, Jr., and Dennis M. Simon, "Promise and Performance: A Dynamic Model of Presidential Popularity," *American Political Science Review* (June 1985), 79:334–358.

7. Robert S. Strauss, "What's Right with U.S. Campaigns," *Foreign Policy* (Summer 1984), p. 8.

8. In mid-August 1984, for example, 47 percent vs. 35 percent of the public thought Mondale would be better than Reagan at "keeping the country out of war." At the same time, 51 percent vs. 28 percent felt that Reagan would be better at "making people proud to be Americans" and 48 percent vs. 34 percent said he would be better at "increasing respect for the United States overseas." George H. Gallup, *The Gallup Poll: Public Opinion, 1984* (Wilmington, Del.: Scholarly Resources, 1985), p. 984.

9. For a historical overview of U.S. attitudes toward Russia see Thomas A. Bailey, *American Faces Russia: Russian and American Relations From Early Times to Our Day* (Ithaca: Cornell University Press, 1950).

10. George H. Gallup, *The Gallup Poll: Public Opinion, 1935–1972* (New York: Random House, 1972), p. 1087.

11. See, for example, Asher, *Presidential Elections and American Politics*, pp. 119–120.

12. George H. Gallup, *The Gallup Poll: Public Opinion, 1972–1977* (Wilmington, Del.: Scholarly Resource, 1978), p. 64.

13. See Gerald M. Pomper, *Elections in America: Control and Influence in Democratic Politics* (New York: Dodd, Mead, 1968), p. 251.

14. Ibid., p. 255.

15. *The Gallup Poll: Public Opinion, 1972–1977*, p. 2136.

16. Stanley Kelley, Jr., *Interpreting Elections* (Princeton: Princeton University Press, 1983), chapter 5.

17. See Douglas A. Hibbs, *The American Political Economy: Macroeconomics and Electoral Politics in the United States* (Cambridge: Harvard University Press, 1987); Gerald Kramer, "Short Term Fluctuations in U.S. Voting Behavior: 1896–1964," *American Political Science Review* (1971), 65:131–145; Edward Tufte, *Political Control of the Economy* (New Haven: Yale University Press, 1978).

18. Clyde H. Farnsworth, "When Running for President It's Hard to Be Free on Trade," *New York Times*, October 9, 1988.

19. In this case the partisan struggle was compounded by personal differences between the two presidential candidates.

20. Arthur S. Link, *Wilson the Diplomatist* (Baltimore: Johns Hopkins University Press, 1957).

21. Thomas Halper, *Foreign Policy Crisis: Appearance and Reality in Decision Making* (Columbus, Ohio: Merrill, 1971), p. 312.

22. Quoted in Ronald Steel, *Imperialists and Other Heroes* (New York: Random House, 1971), p. 119

23. Quoted in Elie Abel, *The Missile Crisis* (Philadelphia: Lippincott, 1969), p. 78. For a view disputing the contention that Kennedy played electoral politics with the missile crisis see Thomas G. Paterson, "Fixation with Cuba: The Bay of Pigs, Missile Crisis, and Covert War Against Fidel Castro," in Thomas G. Paterson, ed., *Kennedy's Quest for Victory: American Foreign Policy, 1961–1963* (New York: Oxford University Press, 1989), pp. 123–155.

24. Kenneth O'Donnell, "LBJ and the Kennedys," *Life*, August 7, 1970, pp. 44–57.

25. I. M. Destler, Leslie H. Gelb, and Anthony Lake, *Our Own Worst Enemy: The Unmaking of American Foreign Policy* (New York: Simon & Schuster, 1984), p. 67.

26. Manfred L. Landecker, "Harry S Truman: Leadership and Public Opinion," in William T. Levantrosser, ed., *Harry S Truman: The Man From Independence* (Westport, Conn.: Greenwood Press, 1986), p. 192.

27. For a discussion of this era see Allen Yarnell, *Democrats and Progressives* (Berkeley: University of California Press, 1974).

28. "Reagan Bids Aides Discuss Issues As Freely As Possible," *New York Times*, January 9, 1981, p. A14.

29. Destler, Gelb, and Lake, *Our Own Worst Enemy*, p. 271.

30. Ibid., p. 11.

31. Alexander Haig, "Alexander Haig," *Time*, April 9, 1984, p. 67.

32. Robert J. Bressler, "The United States and Arms Control," in Robert C. Gray and Stanley J. Michalak, Jr., eds., *American Foreign Policy Since Dtente* (New York: Harper & Row, 1984), p. 35.

33. Schmidt, *Washington Post*, May 5, 1983.

34. Robert Axelrod, *The Evolution of Cooperation* (New York: Basic Books, 1984).

35. Zbigniew Brzezinski, *Power and Principle: Memoirs of a National Security Adviser, 1977–1981* (New York: Farrar, Straus & Giroux, 1983), p. 544.

36. William Quandt, "The Electoral Cycle and the Conduct of Foreign Policy," *Political Science Quarterly* (1986), 101(5):825–836.

37. Townsend Hoopes, *The Devil and John Foster Dulles* (Boston: Little, Brown, 1973), p. 504.

38. On the consequences of election campaigns see Miroslav Nincic, "United States Soviet Policy: The Electoral Connection," *World Politics* (July 1990).

39. See Peter Suedfeld and Philip Tetlock, "Integrative Complexity and Communication in International Crises," *Journal of Conflict Resolution*

(1977), 21(1):169–184, and Philip Tetlock, "Integrative Complexity and American and Soviet Foreign Policy Rhetoric," *Journal of Personality and Social Psychology*, 49(6):1565–1585.

40. Quoted in Yarnell, *Democrats and Progressives*, p. 37.

41. Robert A. Divine, *Foreign Policy and U.S. Presidential Elections: 1952–1960* (New York: New Viewpoints, 1974), p. 33.

42. Ibid., chapter 1.

43. John Lewis Gaddis, *Strategies of Containment: A Critical Appraisal of Postwar American National Security Policy* (New York: Oxford University Press, 1982), p. 127.

44. Ibid., p. 128.

45. See Robert McNamara, *Blundering into Disaster* (New York: Pantheon, 1986), p. 44; also see John Prados, *The Soviet Estimate* (New York: The Dial Press, 1982), pp. 114–115.

46. Reagan is quoted by Gerald Ford in *A Time to Heal: The Autobiography of Gerald R. Ford* (New York: Harper & Row, 1979), p. 337.

47. "Reagan is Stressing a Tough U.S. Stance in Foreign Affairs in Bid to Gain Ground," *Wall Street Journal*, January 31, 1980, p. 8.

48. "Reagan Assails Carter's Policy as Weak," *Wall Street Journal*, January 28, 1980, p. 7

49. "Bentsen Terms Veto of Military Bill Political," *New York Times*, August 7, 1988, p. 24

50. The link between Khrushchev's behavior and U.S. foreign policy is analyzed in Nincic, *Anatomy of Hostility* (San Diego: Harcourt Brace Jovanovich, 1989), chapter 5.

51. Ford, *A Time to Heal*, p. 353.

52. Lawrence Radway, "The Curse of Free Elections," *Foreign Policy* (Fall 1960), p. 70.

53. See Lester W. Milbrath, *Political Participation* (Chicago: Rand McNally, 1965), and Raymond E. Wolfinger and Steven J. Rosenstone, "Who Votes?" paper presented at the annual meeting of the American Political Science Association, Washington, D.C., September 1–4, 1977.

54. Nincic, *Anatomy of Hostility*, chapter 4.

55. Charles W. Ostrom and Brian Job, "The President and the Political Use of Force," *American Political Science Review* (1986), 80(2):541–566.

56. Richard J. Stoll, "The Guns of November: Presidential Reelections and the Use of Force," *Journal of Conflict Resolution* (1984), 28(2):231–246.

57. Philip Tetlock, "Integrative Complexity," pp. 1565–1585.

58. Bruce M. Russett, *Controlling the Sword: The Democratic Governance of National Security* (Cambridge: Harvard University Press, 1990), p. 41.

59. Strauss, "What's Right with U.S. Campaigns," p. 7.

60. Ibid., p. 13.

61. "Report of the President's Commission on Strategic Forces," (Washington, D.C.: Government Printing Office, 1983).
62. Quoted in Walter LaFeber, *American, Russia, and the Cold War: 1945–1984*, 5th ed. (New York: Knopf, 1985), p. 247.
63. V. O. Key, Jr., *Public Opinion and American Democracy* (New York: Knopf, 1961), p. 285.
64. John Burnheim, *Is Democracy Possible? The Alternative to Electoral Politics* (Berkeley: University of California Press, 1985), p. 97.
65. Ibid.

5. Democracy and Deception

1. Woodrow Wilson, *The New Freedom* (Garden City, N.Y.: Doubleday, Page, 1913), p. 113.
2. For a comparatively early and very balanced treatment of the subject see Francis E. Rourke, *Secrecy and Publicity: Dilemmas of Democracy* (Baltimore: Johns Hopkins University Press, 1961); see also Robert E. Goodin, *Manipulatory Politics* (New Haven: Yale University Press, 1980); Morton E. Halperin and Daniel N. Hoffman, *Top Secret: National Security and the Right to Know* (Washington D.C.: New Republic Books, 1977), and J. R. Wriggins, *Freedom or Secrecy* (New York: Oxford University Press, 1964). For a more popular treatment see David Wise, *The Politics of Lying* (New York: Random House, 1973).
3. See *Report of the Congressional Committees Investigating the Iran-Contra Affair with Supplemental Minority and Additional Views* (Washington, D.C.: Government Printing Office, 1987).
4. For a fascinating discussion of a very specific form of secrecy and of its possible implications see Kenneth R. Crispell and Carlo F. Gomez, *Hidden Illness in the White House* (Durham, N.C.: Duke University Press, 1988).
5. Robert Goodin, for one, has argued that "the strategy of secrecy naturally degenerates into the politics of lying, with all the attendant hazards." *Manipulatory Politics*, p. 51. See also Edward A. Shils, *The Torment of Secrecy* (Glencoe, Ill.: Free Press, 1956), especially chapter 6.
6. Good histories of early U.S. involvement in Vietnam are George M. Kahin and John W. Lewis, *The United States in Vietnam*, rev. ed. (New York: Delta, 1969); on the matter of Diem see especially pp. 100–102. See also Stanley Karnow, *Vietnam: A History* (New York: Viking, 1983) and *The Pentagon Papers* (New York: Bantam, 1971).
7. "Transcript of Interview with Ex-Ambassador Lodge on His Return from Vietnam," *New York Time*, June 30, 1964.
8. "Transcript of Remarks by Reagan About Iran," *New York Times*, November 14, 1986.
9. Ibid., p. 14.
10. See, for example, E. Goffman, *The Presentation of Self in Everyday Life* (New York: Doubleday, 1959); R. E. Turner, C. Edgley, and G. Olmstead,

eds., "Information Control in Conversations: Honesty is Not Always the Best Policy," *Kansas Journal of Sociology* (1975), 11:69–89; Karen U. Miller and Abraham Tesser, "Deceptive Behavior in Social Relationships: A Consequence of Violated Expectations," *Journal of Psychology*, 122(3):263–272.

11. For Plato on deception see *The Republic* (New York: Oxford University Press, 1945), chapter 9, especially 389b.

12. Quoted in Sissela Bok, *Lying: Moral Choice in Public and Private Life* (New York: Pantheon, 1978), p. 168.

13. See Anthony Downs, *An Economic Theory of Democracy* (New York: Harper & Row, 1957), chapter 11; also see Gordon Tullock, *Toward a Mathematics of Politics* (Ann Arbor: University of Michigan Press, 1967), chapter 7.

14. See Carl J. Friedrich, *The Pathology of Politics* (New York: Harper & Row, 1972), pp. 177–180.

15. See remarks by Max Frankel, in Bayless Manning et al., "The Role of Secrecy in the Conduct of Foreign Policy," *American Society of International Law: Proceedings* (1972), 66:63.

16. See, for example, Tibor Scitovsky, "Ignorance as a Source of Oligopoly Power," *American Economic Review (Papers and Proceedings)* (May 1950), 40:48–53.

17. Niccolò Machiavelli, *The Prince* [1537] (New York: New American Library, 1952), p. 8.

18. John F. Kennedy, *Public Papers of the President—1961* (Washington, D.C., 1962), p. 336.

19. John Rothchild, "Finding the Facts Bureaucrats Hide," *The Washington Monthly* (January 1972), 3:15.

20. Arthur Sylvester, "The Government Has the Right to Lie," *Saturday Evening Post*, November 18, 1967, p. 10.

21. Quoted in David Wise, *The Politics of Lying*, p. 22.

22. Robert McNamara, *The Essence of Security* (New York: Harper & Row), p. 58.

23. For some of the problems involved in producing an acceptable definition of national security, see Arnold Wolfers, *Discord and Collaboration* (Baltimore: Johns Hopkins University Press, 1962), chapter 10.

24. Gabriel A. Almond, "Public Opinion and National Security Policy," *Public Opinion Quarterly* (Summer 1956), 20:371.

25. Harold Brown, *Thinking About National Security: Defense and Foreign Policy in a Dangerous World* (Boulder, Colo.: Westview Press, 1983), p. 4.

26. Richard V. Allen, "Foreign Policy and National Security: The White House Perspective," in Richard N. Holwill, ed., *Agenda '83: A Mandate for Leadership Report* (Washington D.C.: The Heritage Foundation, 1983), p. 6.

27. Arthur Selwin Miller, "Implications of Watergate: Some Proposals for Cutting the Presidency Down to Size," *Hastings Constitutional Law Quarterly* (Winter 1975), 2:52–54.

28. "Nixon Concedes White House Effort to Conceal Some Aspects of Watergate: Cites Concern Over National Security," *New York Times*, May 23, 1973, p. A1.

29. Hans J. Morgenthau, *American Foreign Policy* (London: Methuen, 1952), p. 224.

30. Ibid., p. 229.

31. It is also useful to contemplate the wisdom of Thomas Jefferson's observation, "I know of no safe depository of the ultimate powers of the society but the people themselves; and if we think them not enlightened enough to exercise their control with a wholesome discretion, the remedy is not to take it from them but to inform their discretion." In Andrew A. Lipscomb and Albert Ellery Bergh, eds., *The Writings of Thomas Jefferson*, 15 vols. (Washington, D.C.: The Thomas Jefferson Memorial Association, 1904), 15:278.

32. "Two U.S. Aides Visit Peking in Month After the Killings," *New York Times*, December 19, 1989, p. A1.

33. Nicholas de B. Katzenbach, "Foreign Policy, Public Opinion, and Secrecy," *Foreign Affairs* (October 1973), 52:8

34. Ibid., p. 9.

35. Subcommittee on Separation of Powers, Senate Judiciary Committee, *Executive Privilege: The Withholding of Information by the Executive*, Hearings, 92d Cong., 1st sess., 1971 (Washington, D.C.: Government Printing Office, 1972), p. 347.

36. Arthur M. Schlesinger, Jr., *The Imperial Presidency* (Boston: Houghton Mifflin, 1973), p. 361.

37. Samuel P. Huntington, *American Politics: The Promise of Disharmony* (Cambridge: Harvard University Press, 1981), p. 81.

38. James Madison, *Journal of the Federal Convention*, ed. E. H. Scott (Chicago: Albert Scott, 1894), p. 58

39. Sissela Bok, *Secrets: On the Ethics of Concealment and Revelation* (New York: Pantheon, 1982), p. 175. See also Harold Wilensky, *Organizational Intelligence: Knowledge and Policy in Government and Industry* (New York: Basic Books, 1967), p. 138.

40. "Excerpts from Remarks by President to Gathering of Former Prisoners of War," *New York Times*, May 25, 1973, p. 16.

41. See Peter A. French, *Ethics in Government* (New York: Prentice Hall, 1983), pp. 121–124.

42. Bok, *Secrets*, p. 181.

43. The concept does not correspond to that of *inherent*, as opposed to delegated, powers. The argument for inherent powers is based on the sov-

ereignty of the United States under international law and the executive duties
that naturally inhere in this sovereignty. In the case of inherent power there
is no necessary assumption of public consent, whether explicit or implied.

44. H. H. Gerth and C. Wright Mills, eds., *From Max Weber: Essays in
Sociology* (New York: Oxford University Press, 1946), p. 223.

45. Robert Goodin maintains that when "national security" is invoked
as a cover for secrecy, the "claim is usually an outright and often transparent
lie perpetrated for bureaucratic advantage." *Manipulatory Politics*, p. 50.

46. I. M. Destler, *Presidents, Bureaucrats, and Foreign Policy* (Princeton:
Princeton University Press, 1974), p. 66.

47. According to Adam Yarmolinsky and Gregory D. Foster, *Paradoxes
of Power* (Bloomington: Indiana University Press, 1983), p. 38.

48. Hedrick Smith, *The Power Game: How Washington Works* (New
York: Random House, 1988), p. 634.

49. These aspects of the Iran-Contra affair are described in Michael A.
Ledeen, *Perilous Statecraft: An Insider's Account of the Iran-Contra Affair*
(New York: Scribner's, 1988), and Alex Whiting, *Covert Operations and the
Democratic Process: the Implications of the Iran-Contra Affair* (Washing-
ton, D.C.: Center for National Security Studies, 1987); see also Theodore
Draper, *A Very Thin Line: The Iran-Contra Affair* (New York: Hill and
Wang, 1991).

50. Hedrick Smith reports on a number of interviews with key participants on this issue in *The Power Game*, pp. 603–609.

51. Quoted in *Parade*, September 26, 1971.

52. "U.S. Policy on Terror," *New York Times*, November 11, 1986, p.
A10.

53. Margaret G. Hermann and Charles F. Hermann, "Who Makes Foreign
Policy Decisions and How: An Empirical Inquiry," *International Studies
Quarterly* (1989), 33:361–387.

54. See, for example, Hans J. Morgenthau, *Politics Among Nations: The
Struggle for Power and Peace*, 6th ed. (New York: Knopf, 1985), pp. 164–
168.

55. Richard Cheney, *Iran Contra Hearings*, July 20, 1987.

56. Doris Kearns, *Lyndon Johnson and the American Dream* (New York:
Harper & Row, 1976).

6. In Search of the National Interest

1. Two particularly useful statements on the role of ethical norms in the
conduct of international relations are in Stanley Hoffmann, *Duties Beyond
Borders: On the Limits and Possibilities of Ethical International Politics*
(Syracuse: Syracuse University Press, 1981), and Michael J. Smith, "Moral
Reasoning and Moral Responsibility in International Relations," in Kenneth

W. Thompson, ed., *Ethics and International Relations* (New Brunswick: Transaction Books, 1985), pp. 33–38.

2. An early argument to this effect was advanced in Thomas I. Cook and Malcolm Moos, *Power Through Purpose: The Realism of Idealism as a Basis for Foreign Policy* (Baltimore: Johns Hopkins University Press, 1954); see also Charles Frankel, *Human Rights and Foreign Policy* (New York: Foreign Policy Association, 1978), and Alan Tonelson, "Human Rights: The Bias We Need," *Foreign Policy* (Winter 1982–83), 49:52–74.

3. Edward H. Alden and Franz Schurmann, *Why We Need Ideologies in American Foreign Policy* (Berkeley: Institute of International Studies, 1990), pp. 14–15.

4. Donald E. Nuechterlein, *National Interests and Presidential Leadership: the Setting of Priorities* (Boulder, Colo.: Westview Press, 1978), p. 5.

5. Robert E. Osgood, *Ideals and Self-Interest in America's Foreign Relations* (Chicago: University of Chicago Press, 1953) p. 4.

6. Hans J. Morgenthau, *Politics Among Nations: The Struggle for Power and Peace*, 6th ed. (New York: Knopf, 1948), p. 5.

7. Ibid., p. 29.

8. Ibid., p. 37.

9. Morgenthau, *Politics Among Nations*, pp. 5–7.

10. Raymond Aron, *Peace and War: A Theory of International Relations* (New York: Doubleday, 1966), p. 90.

11. Arnold Wolfers, *Discord and Collaboration* (Baltimore: Johns Hopkins University Press, 1961), especially chapter 10.

12. George F. Kennan, "Lectures on Foreign Policy," *Illinois Law Review* (1951), 45:723.

13. Ibid., p. 730

14. Stephen Krasner, *Defending the National Interest* (Princeton: Princeton University Press, 1978), chapters 1–2.

15. Ibid., pp. 11–12.

16. Ibid., p. 43.

17. Osgood, *Ideals and Self-Interest*, pp. 5–7.

18. Ibid., p. 6.

19. Paul Kennedy, *The Rise and Fall of the Great Powers* (New York: Random House, 1987).

20. Aron, *Peace and War*, pp. 73–76.

21. For example, Nuechterlein, *National Interests and Presidential Leadership*, p. 5.

22. Kennan, for example, has explicitly excluded ideological goals from his notion of the national interest, e.g., "Morality and Foreign Policy," *Foreign Affairs* (Winter 1985–86), pp. 205–219.

23. Alexander L. George and Robert O. Keohane, "The Concept of the National Interest," pp. 223–225, in Alexander L. George, *Presidential De-*

cisionmaking in Foreign Policy: The Effective Use of Information and Advice (Boulder, Colo.: Westview Press, 1980), pp. 217–238.

24. I have discussed the economic consequences of defense spending in Miroslav Nincic, *The Arms Race: The Political Economy of Military Growth* (New York: Praeger, 1982), especially chapter 3.

25. Bruce M. Russett and Elizabeth C. Hanson, *Interest and Ideology: The Foreign Policy Beliefs of American Businessmen* (San Francisco: W. H. Freeman, 1975), pp. 70–72.

26. Reported in "Bosses Favor Trimming Defense but Oppose Any Delay in Tax Cuts," *Wall Street Journal*, April 13, 1982.

27. "Business Chiefs See Need to Cut Military Spending to Trim Deficits," *New York Times*, October 11, 1982, p. A1; see also "Executives Bid Reagan Cut Deficit," *New York Times*, March 13, 1982, p. D1.

28. Charles A. Beard, *The Open Door at Home* (New York: 1935), pp. v–vi.

29. This point is developed in Edward L. Morse, *Modernization and the Transformation of International Relations* (New York: Free Press, 1976), especially chapter 4.

30. See, for example, James N. Rosenau, "National Interest," *International Encyclopedia of Social Sciences*, 2 vols. (New York: Macmillan, 1968), 2:34–40.

31. Raymond Aron, *Peace and War*, p. 91.

32. James G. March and Herbert A. Simon, *Organizations* (New York: John Wiley, 1958), pp. 155–158; see also George, *Presidential Decisionmaking*, p. 219.

33. Note the difference between this conception and Krasner's.

INDEX